Empire Eternal: In Defense of Imperialism
Sinclair Jenkins

EMPIRE ETERNAL

In Defense of Imperialism

BY

SINCLAIR JENKINS

ANTELOPE HILL PUBLISHING

This work contains a collection of writings, many of which were originally published by the author on *American Renaissance* (amren.com). Publication dates have been specified for these writings where applicable. Some minor edits have been made from these original publications.

Publisher's Note: Antelope Hill is proud to publish various and at times differing perspectives which contribute to understanding the history of the European people, building their political consciousness, or demonstrating the intellect of contemporary White writers and thinkers. The relationship between the White race as a collective life and the concept of imperialism has sometimes been tense, and the imperialist reach of European blood throughout the earth has proceeded from differing motivations, some more or less noble, some more or less beneficial for Whites themselves. Regardless of the greater circumstances, the stories in this book are moments in history that demonstrate the martial prowess and courage of European men of action.

Cover art by Swifty
Edited by Taylor Young
Formatted by Margaret Bauer

Antelope Hill Publishing
antelopehillpublishing.com

Paperback ISBN-13: 978-1-956887-36-5
EPUB ISBN-13: 978-1-953730-22-0

CONTENTS

Introduction

Why imperialism? That question must be addressed. After all, for many on the right-wing of the spectrum, imperialism is the obvious enemy. American neoliberal imperialism has a stranglehold on the world, and every tendril of the monster oozes the grease of sexual depravity, homosexual and transsexual "rights," minority privileges, and fawning adoration of the marketplace. If you care about European and American advocacy, then you would, in Anno Domini 2021, be an anti-imperialist or at least against the global leviathan of Washington, DC.

First of all, the American nation and its founding stock would not exist if it were not for imperialism. Rather than the US Constitution or even the Mayflower Compact, the true founding document of the American people is Richard Hakluyt's *A Discourse Concerning Western Planting* (1584). In that work and other pamphlets, the English patriot Hakluyt laid bare the many reasons why London should establish colonies (or "plantations") in the New World much as had already been done in Ireland. Hakluyt argued that:

> *The Queen of England's title to all the West Indies, or at the least to as much as is from Florida to the Circle arctic, is more lawful and right than the Spaniards or any other Christian Princes. . . .*

> *That speedy planting in diverse fit places is most necessary upon these lucky western discoveries for fear of the danger of being prevented by other nations which have the like intentions, with the order thereof and other reasons therewithal alleged.*[1]

Hakluyt's propaganda found a receptive audience in Queen Elizabeth I as well as the poet-explorer-privateer Sir Walter Raleigh. Inspired by Hakluyt's words, as well as the common English belief in the sheer barbarism of Spanish colonialism in the New World, Raleigh and his followers established the earliest English colonies in North America. These attempts would be succeeded by the permanent colonies in Virginia established by the Virginia Company of London. It is here, in the late sixteenth century, that the American spirit, with its Anglo roots, is first given expression in the mixture of idealism, adventure, and efficiency. In essence, the genus and germ of American nationalism is English imperialism.

There are those on the Dissident Right who articulate support for absolutist nationalism. Men like RAMZPAUL believe in nationalism for all races and peoples. Built into this belief system is the conceit that Euro-American identitarianism should only concern itself with the preservation of European homelands. This is a worthy cause. Indeed, in our age it is one of the few causes worth dying for. However, this brand of nationalist identitarianism is still a retreat—a philosophical surrender to forces of neoliberalism and Third World-ism. It is a surrender of the hands and a collective shout of: Just leave us alone!

The left will never leave us alone. The left is always hungry for more power. It is never satisfied. That is why fighting it is a necessity. Restoring imperialism is but one weapon to wield in this fight. However, this book seeks to show how it is the strongest, most proactive weapon.

Empire Eternal, which you hold in your hands now, is an attempt to show that the age of imperialism and colonialism was the apex of Euro-American civilization. My point in these essays, almost all of which are purely historical in nature and substance, is to reaffirm the glory of a European and American-led world order. In a similar way, this book seeks to argue that a return to imperialism would be a boon for Europeans and Americans, and indeed the rest of the world.

The stark truth facing us in the twenty-first century is that there are only two options: globalist hegemony led by China and Euro-American turncoats, or neo-imperialism led by nation-states. The former are akin to robber barons, who take and take without giving anything in return. The forces of global and neoliberal capital have no allegiance to the nation-state or their people, that is unless the nation-state in question is China (for more information on China's desire for revenge against the West, see "The Chinese Uprising Against Whites"). Imperialists at the very least mostly provided their fellow citizens with the benefits of other lands. If they did not, then the drive for conquest would not last. Imperial states are also beholden to national voters; the same cannot be said of transnational corporations. There will never be an age of harmonious cooperation. This goes against human nature, and it always irritates large and powerful civilizations, which are built for conquest and expansion. Imperialism generates pride, new opportunities, and incredible vitality. Globalism provides nothing of value except to the elite few who can reap its rewards.

There is no hate here. The only emotion is pride—pride in Christendom, pride in our forefathers, and pride in the much maligned colonization system that gave the world the greatest creole civilizations ever known, from the Old South to the Viceroyalty of New Spain. The men who founded these great civilizations are long gone, but their blood still lives within us. We are called to conquer. Our age, like every other age, is a war of all against all for the domination of space. In addition, to paraphrase the great Bronze Age Pervert, the war for space knows no strategic alliances. No Black, Asian, or Latino nationalist will ever lift a finger for our movement. We are on our own, thank God. Therefore, let these essays inspire you to seek out adventure in distant lands, or stand fast in the arena of politics and proclaim your allegiance to a Greater Euro-American Order.

I would like to thank Jared Taylor and the editors at *American Renaissance* for publishing so many of these articles. To you all I owe a debt that can never be repaid. Finally, I would like to thank every editor that I have ever worked with, every friend I have made along the way, and every member of my extended family who has shed his or her blood for the maintenance of Christendom and the European-American world order. Although you wore diverse uniforms, from Confederate gray and Union blue to khaki and the soiled linen of Jamestown, your sacrifices mattered and still matter.

---

[1] Richard Hakluyt, *A Discourse Concerning Western Planting, Written in the Year 1584,* Charles Deane, ed. (Cambridge, MA: Press of J. Wilson, 1877): 1–5.

American Renaissance, June 26th, 2020.

European minorities are often prone to the "bunker mentality." Colonel Reginald Dyer, the Anglo-Indian commander of mostly Gurkha and Muslim troops during the Amritsar Massacre of 1919, has been pathologized by generations of armchair psychologists as an example of the bunker mentality because he had grown up as White minority in British India. Dyer and others of his ilk grew up with tales of the Sepoy Mutiny and the Bibighar Massacre, where the survivors of Cawnpore, almost all of whom were women and children, were slaughtered by local butchers under the command of a prostitute named Nana Saheb.[1] The *pied noirs* of French Algeria had a similar outlook; today's White South Africans do too.

In colonial New England, the Puritans, who mostly clung to the Atlantic coastline, had a similar disposition. Their enemies came in many forms: the French in Canada and their Native American proxies, the Dutch in New York and their Native American proxies, the tribes of New England like the powerful Narragansett, and the assorted "devils" that haunted the uncivilized forests. King Philip's War (1676–1678) was the explosion of racial violence that the Puritans long feared. The New Englanders won, but at a cost of approximately 800 dead out of an overall population of 52,000 (a death rate of 1,538 per 100,000).[2]

As with all historical events, there is a debate over what caused King Philip's War. The war saw conflict between new generations of leaders, both Indian and European. Metacom (aka King Philip) belonged to Wampanoag royalty. His father, Massasoit, brokered an era of long peace between his tribe and the New Englanders after extending goodwill to the Plymouth Colony after its establishment in 1620.[3] Massasoit's death coincided with the deaths of the first generation of New England leaders in Plymouth, Massachusetts Bay, and Connecticut. English desire for land, as well as underhanded business practices such as plying Indians with alcohol, have also been named as the deciding factor. Philip, as a new sachem, made alliances with other Algonquin-speaking tribes in order to resist New England encroachment.[4]

The immediate cause of the war stemmed from the murder of John Sassamon, a Christian convert and a councilor alongside Philip at the Taunton Agreement in 1671. Another Christian Indian, Patuckson, told Plymouth Colony officials that Sassamon's murder stemmed from his decision to warn the English about Philip's intention to begin an offensive war. [5] Plymouth tried the accused killers. Twelve New Englanders and an auxiliary jury of Indians found the defendants guilty. For King Philip and his tribal alliance, this was the opening salvo. On June 20th, 1675, a band of Pokanoket attacked the Plymouth settlement of Swansea.[6]

The war itself featured small-scale ambushes and town and village attacks. When Indian raiders showed up in New England towns with English-made muskets, the residents more often than not sought refuge in garrison houses or fortified blockhouses. This resulted in the burning or destruction of half of all towns between Maine (then part of the Massachusetts Bay) and southern Connecticut.[7] The New England Confederation's army relied on small militia units organized at the colony and town level:

By 1675, Massachusetts alone had some seventy-three organized companies. Each county maintained a dozen foot companies and one cavalry, while the counties of Suffolk, Middlesex, and Essex fielded a combined cavalry company. Each foot company contained about seventy privates and each cavalry about fifty. Muster days were held on a regular basis, although drilling could not compensate for the fact that New England's defense was dependent on farmers unaccustomed to wilderness warfare.[8]

Indeed, it is worth remembering the quality and character of the people who settled New England. Historian David Hackett Fischer shows that New England's Puritans came predominately from East Anglia, a unique region of eastern England claimed by the Jutes and where the heretical Lollards and other Reformation schismatics enjoyed power not seen elsewhere in the country.[9] The families that settled New England did not settle as warriors, but as religiously-minded merchants. John Winthrop, the leader of the Massachusetts Bay and the man with the power to make decisions regarding violence, was himself a poor shot according to biographer Edmund Morgan. Like their English brethren in Virginia, New Englanders hoped to establish a peaceful and Protestant state in America that would be bi-racial and harmonious. They did not want to repeat the supposed evils of the Spanish in Mexico and South America, where Indians were killed and African slaves were imported to do hard labor.[10] This idealism evaporated with the Jamestown Massacre of 1622; King Philip's War ended idealism in New England. The war became one of ethnic cleansing.

For the most part, the New England Confederation could not lead and proved to be inept at winning the war against King Philip's insurgency. Plymouth and the colonies in Connecticut chafed under centralized rule from Boston, while the New England militiamen often went home after fruitless patrols in the New England hinterlands. The one pitched battle of the entire conflict came during the Great Swamp Fight of December 1675. Here, about 1,000 militiamen from Massachusetts Bay, Plymouth, and Connecticut "attacked a large, fortified Narragansett village located in the Great Swamp (present-day South Kingston, Rhode Island)."[11] The New Englanders won the day, killing almost 100 hundred warriors. However, the battle brought the mighty Narragansett into the war, which spelled doom for Rhode Island (which never wanted the war). In the northern theater of Maine, the Wabanaki and their allies killed as many as 400 settlers and drove the New Englanders out of every settlement except for Casco and a few other coastal enclaves.

In terms of leadership, the New Englanders had only two competent commanders: Major Richard Waldron and Captain

Benjamin Church. These men approached the war differently. Waldron was a rigid Puritan and one of the founders of Dover, New Hampshire (then part of the Massachusetts Bay). An experienced soldier, but brutal to Indians, Waldron oversaw the many tit-for-tat battles in Maine and New Hampshire. His militiamen sought pitched battles with their foes. Church, on the other hand, came from Plymouth Colony, worked as a carpenter, and speculated in land in Rhode Island. Church believed in maneuverability. Unlike other New England leaders, Church also believed in using Indian allies and training his New England militiamen to fight like Indians. Church's force would be the first ever Ranger unit in American history. Church's small band of fighters finally killed King Philip in August 1676, thus essentially ending the war.

Benjamin Church is often seen as the preeminent figure of the war because he left behind a diary. This diary, besides detailing Church's friendly relations with Indians (including a possibly sexual relationship with a female sachem) and his frustrations with the Puritan establishment in Boston, became one of the most popular documents in the Early American Republic. According to literature professor Philip Gould, Church's diary was emblematic of the Early Republic's search for "virtue" and "republicanism." In short, from the Revolution to the age of Jackson, Church was upheld as the quintessential American: a carpenter who grabbed his gun in order to protect his civilization.[12] Church would later serve in King William's War (1688–1697) and Queen Anne's War (1702–1713) until dying at age seventy-eight (some sources say seventy-nine).

Whereas Church's diary is filled with information about troop movements, sit-downs with Indians, and the like, King Philip's War also produced another eyewitness account. Mary Rowlandson of Lancaster, Massachusetts was captured by Indian raiders on February 10th, 1675. Her captivity lasted for eleven weeks and five days.[13] During that time Rowlandson and her fellow New England captives endured treks through the Massachusetts frontier, southern Vermont, and New Hampshire. Rowlandson's diary, later published as *The Narrative of the Captivity and Restoration of Mrs. Mary Rowlandson*, became an early best-seller. She details how attacking Indians killed her entire family before kidnapping her and her six-year-old daughter, Sarah.

> *But out we must go, the fire increasing, and coming along behind us, roaring, and the Indians gaping before us with their guns, spears, and hatchets, to devour us. No sooner were we out of the house, but my brother-in-law (being before wounded, in defending the house, in or near the throat) fell down dead, whereat the Indians scornfully shouted, hallooed, and were presently upon him, stripping off his clothes.[14]*

Sarah would tragically die during captivity. Rowlandson's deliverance would come thanks to the women of Boston who purchased her ransom. Although made a slave to an Indian leader and forced to listen to her captors describe the killing of New England militiamen, Rowlandson was at least spared the fate of colonial New England's other famous heroine, Anne Hutchinson. After being banished from Boston for preaching Antinomianism, Hutchinson and her family relocated to New Netherland. There, in the summer of 1643, Anne and her entire family were scalped by an Algonquian tribe during Kieft's War (1643–1645). The tribe sought revenge on Dutch settlers, but wound up killing English ones instead.

The story of King Philip's War is the story of American survival. Despite Jill Lepore's lazy assertion in *The Name of War: King Philip's War and the Origins of American Identity*, the war did not see New Englanders develop a separate identity as Americans. If anything, after the war, English America moved closer to the metropole. England returned the favor by sending more government officials and curtailing the liberties that had been established by the original charters. Indeed, by the time of the American Revolution, Americans in the North and South saw themselves as British and happily invoked King George III and the traditions of monarchy against the illegal activities of the Parliament in London. No, the lesson of King Philip's War is not that it created a separate American identity, but that it established

New England as a thoroughly English civilization. No tribal alliance would never again seriously threaten Massachusetts or Connecticut, thus allowing for the full flowering of Anglo-Saxon culture on these shores.

Most important of all, the key lesson of King Philip's War is that every inch of New England, and indeed America, was fought over and won by the Historic American Nation. The Puritans suffered tremendous loses, but ultimately managed to win the day by defending their towns and innovating new ways of warfare (rangering). The next time some rioting Antifa type or racial grievance brigade member says that their people "built this country," remind them of King Philip's War and tell them: No, we fought for it and died for it, and it will always be our civilization.

[1] Mimi Matthews, "The Bibighar Massacre: The Darkest Days of the Indian Rebellion of 1857," *Mimi Matthews.com*, 2018 Dec. 6.
[2] Eric B. Schultz and Michael J. Tougias, *King Philip's War: The History and Legacy of America's Forgotten Conflict* (New York: The Countryman Press, 2017): 5.
[3] Schultz and Tougias, 1.
[4] Philip Gould, "Reinventing Benjamin Church: Virtue, Citizenship and the History of King Philip's War in Early National America," *Journal of the Early Republic*, Vol. 16, No. 4 (Winter, 1996): 645.
[5] Schultz and Tougias, 27.
[6] Ibid., 2.
[7] Gould, "Reinventing Benjamin Church," 645.
[8] Schultz and Tougias, 21.
[9] David Hackett Fischer, *Albion's Seed: Four British Folkways in America* (Oxford and New York: Oxford University Press, 1989): 46.
[10] Alan Gallay, *Walter Ralegh: Architect of Empire* (New York: Basic Books, 2019): 6.
[11] Schultz and Tougias, 53.
[12] Gould, "Reinventing Benjamin Church," 648.
[13] Schultz and Tougias, 341.
[14] Qtd. in Schultz and Tougias, 343.

American Renaissance, July 17th, 2020.

Back before America became a nation of self-hating post-nationalists, our civilization believed in Manifest Destiny. First uttered in 1845 by John L. O'Sullivan, the founder and editor of the *United States Democratic Review* in New York, the notion of Manifest Destiny envisioned a United States that connected the Pacific and the Atlantic. Manifest Destiny similarly believed that "white Anglo-Saxons . . . were preordained to spread civilization across the vast continent for the sake of its cultural and economic advancement." [1] Manifest Destiny was, in a sense, a Yankee version of Venezuelan revolutionary Simon Bolivar's pan-Americanism.

Perhaps no figure embodied the spirit of Manifest Destiny like the "gray-eyed man of destiny," William Walker. Barely remembered in the United States, Walker is today reviled in Central America. The Marxist *Sandinistas* of Nicaragua (whose politics have been praised by Senator Bernie Sanders) instruct their children about how Walker was the first Yankee "imperialist" to invade their tranquil home.[2] A film about Walker was released in 1987. Directed by British leftist Mr. Alex Cox, *Walker* is a surreal send-up of Washington's then current involvement in the civil war in Nicaragua and elsewhere in Latin America. Cox turned Walker into a gaslit Rambo or a more venomous, less satirical *Mr. Freedom*. This is the general view of Walker: a bogeyman and a pirate hellbent on turning Latin America into series of US protectorates.

But was William Walker truly the embodiment of the "unique evil" of American imperialism? In some ways, Walker was an American Alexander the Great, with a private army called the

American Phalanx. Walker's designs for Central America were far greater than Manifest Destiny too, with Walker aspiring to create an independent republic uniting Nicaragua, Honduras, Guatemala, and El Salvador.3 The Walker story is complicated, full of incredible heroics and terrible betrayals of justice, and has a legacy that has endured in subtle ways up to the present.

Born on May 8th, 1824 as the first of six children to Scottish immigrant James S. Walker and his Kentucky-born bride Mary Norvell Walker, William Walker grew up in the frontier city of Nashville, Tennessee. The Walker family belonged to Nashville's commercial upper crust, with the elder Walker making his fortune in steamboats. 4 Other members of the family were equally distinguished: maternal grandfather Lipscomb Norvell was a veteran of the Continental Army who fought at Trenton and Monmouth, while several of William's uncles and cousins fought the British during the War of 1812 or the Mexicans during the Texas Revolution. The family was a proud and illustrious one, and young William never went hungry nor did he ever experience deprivations of any kind.

The eldest Walker child proved intelligent and dedicated to his studies. He enrolled at the University of Nashville at age of thirteen. There he studied Greek, Latin, trigonometry, international law, medicine, and other subjects. Walker also participated in the Agatheridan Society (a literary debate club) and proved to be a devout Christian. He graduated summa cum laude in October 1838 at the ripe age of fourteen. From there Walker matriculated at the University of Pennsylvania, where he studied medicine. In 1843, after completing his studies with a dissertation on the human iris, Walker traveled throughout Europe thanks to a generous allowance from his family. Walker spent the better part of two years in Paris, which helped him to recognize the superiority of American notions of individual liberty over the "popish" tendencies of the French.5

Upon returning to the United States, Walker decided to alter his career path by switching to law. He began by studying the Tennessee law code under Nashville attorney James Whitworth. Then, after giving up Nashville for New Orleans, Walker committed to memory French civil codes, which continue to serve as the founding principles of Louisiana law. Soon enough Walker offered his legal services to the citizens of the Crescent City, but few seemed interested. This required another career change, and by 1849, Walker owned a share in the *Daily Crescent* newspaper. As editor, Walker's *Daily Crescent* took a moderate line on the issue of slavery. The paper was more noteworthy for its contentious and very public battles with rival newspaper, the *Delta*.

It is not known for sure when and where Walker became enamored with the idea of military adventurism, but the idea of "filibustering," or mercenary work, was then popular in the United States. In 1819, James Long of Tennessee, after serving in the US Army during the War of 1812, took several volunteers from Natchez, Mississippi, and with the backing of that city's merchant class, tried to conquer Mexican Texas. The Long Expedition ended in dismal failure. Texas became an independent republic thanks to American settlers who formed self-defense militias to protect their lives and property from both marauding Comanches and eventually the Mexican Army. While Walker lived in New Orleans, Americans in both the North and South voiced support for Cuban revolutionary Narciso Lopez, who used American filibusters during several botched attempts to wrest Cuba from the Spanish crown. Before his execution at the hands of Spanish authorities, Lopez's chief desire was to see Cuba annexed by the United States, preferably as a slave-owning state.[6]

Walker clearly harbored dreams of adventure. This would explain why, before the age of thirty and without military training of any kind, he organized the short-lived conquest of the Mexican state of Sonora. In 1853, Walker and about one hundred men left San Francisco for Baja California. They told the US government that they planned on working in the mines of Sonora, but in reality, the men carried rifles, pistols, and knives instead of pickaxes. At the time, Northern Mexico was a desolate place where roving Apache bands terrorized villagers and the wealthy *rancheros* alike. The corrupt central government in Mexico City could not do much about it except offer generous settlement grants to foreigners, especially German and French settlers who were seen as more trustworthy than land-hungry Yankees.

Walker justified his military adventure as a civilizing mission designed to protect innocent Mexicans from the ravages of Apache raids. Not long after leaving the commercial ship *Caroline*, Walker's small war band took the city of La Paz without much of a fight. From there, the First Independent Battalion (the name Walker gave to his army) marched into the desert. Their new country, the Republic of Lower California, was declared free and sovereign of Mexico. By November 1853, the Republic of Lower California was renamed as the Republic of Sonora. Walker became the first president and instituted the Civil Code of Louisiana as the new state's law. Tellingly, this meant that the Republic of Sonora legalized slavery while it remained illegal in the rest of Mexico. This was never put in practice, as Walker's professed claim to control all of Sonora and the Baja Peninsula was not based on reality.[7]

The independent Republic of Sonora would only last until May 1854. Despite enjoying a recruiting office in San Francisco, Walker's army never amounted to much. These mostly untrained volunteers engaged in more looting than fighting, and when they did fight, they tended to skirmish with a hodgepodge of local Mexican militia, Indian warriors, and professional soldiers. Arguably Walker's most powerful enemy was the administration of President Franklin Pierce, which saw Walker's actions as at best a nuisance and at worst a direct violation of America's Neutrality Act of 1818. Walker would be charged with violations of the Neutrality Act in San Francisco after his Republic of Sonora fell due to a combination of military resistance led by Sonoran rancher Antonio Maria Melendrez and political pressure by General John E. Wool, the head of US forces on the Pacific coast.[8] The final remnants of Walker's ragtag army surrendered to the US Army in San Diego. If the US government hoped that the failure of the Republic of Sonora would stop Walker from pursuing future filibustering campaigns, he proved them wrong almost immediately.

Besides Panama, the other Central American country prized by American industrialists was Nicaragua. Thanks to many inland waterways, including the San Juan River that empties into the Caribbean at San Juan del Norte, men like Cornelius Vanderbilt dreamed of building a canal in Nicaragua to link the Atlantic and Pacific. Even without a canal, American companies like the Pacific Mail Steamship Company and especially the Accessory Transit Company made good money moving men and supplies across Nicaragua. As a result, Nicaragua's port cities and inland trading posts had a sizable American community in the 1850s. No city boasted of more Americans than Greytown on the Atlantic coast, which belonged to the Mosquito Kingdom, a protectorate of the British Empire ruled by English-speaking Indians.

The biggest problem with making money in Nicaragua was the country's terminal civil strife. Ever since declaring independence from Spain, Nicaragua had been fought over by the Legitimist conservatives based in the city of Granada and the Liberals headquartered in Leon. As much a familial and municipal feud as a political one, the cycle of civil wars between the Legitimists and Liberals would last well into the twentieth century and require several US military interventions.[9] Thanks to an election in 1853 that produced no single majority, Nicaragua devolved into civil war once again. From their sanctuary in Honduras, the Liberals under the leadership of Francisco Castellon and Maximo Jerez sought foreign volunteers for their army. Many Americans answered the call, including Walker. After selling his shares in the San Francisco *Commercial Advertiser* newspaper, Walker and two San Francisco notables approached Castellon and reached an agreement whereby the Americans were given 21,000 acres of land and military wages provided that they could recruit and command an army of 300 men against Granada.[10] Walker took command of this force, the American Phalanx, and although its first incarnation stood at barely over 150 men, it was sent into battle immediately. The bloody birth of the Phalanx occurred at the First Battle of Rivas, where an initially successful American charge was repulsed by the Legitimist defenders. Several of Walker's officers were killed in the repeated attempts to overrun the barricades at Rivas.

Not deterred by their failure at Rivas, the Phalanx moved back to the Pacific coast where they enjoyed the use of several commandeered ships. Thanks to his independent command, Walker followed a different plan from the one preferred by his

Liberal peers. Walker recognized that controlling the river routes to the ocean was vital as it not only allowed him to pillage the supply depots controlled by the Accessory Transit Company (therefore showing the lie in the left-wing belief that Walker was an agent of American capital and financial interests), but it also allowed for new volunteers to be safely shipped in from New Orleans, San Francisco, and New York. According to his own records, Walker's Phalanx in Nicaragua between January and April 1857 included 1,072 soldiers (excluding 250 officers). Of this a majority were from New York (174) and Louisiana (77), and most had signed up for service in San Francisco (189).[11] Given this fact, the myth that Walker was the vanguard of Southern expansionism is untenable as most of his men came from non-slaveholding regions of the US.

Barring a few veterans of the Mexican American War and professional mercenaries like Charles Henningsen, the Phalanx relied on raw recruits supplied with their own weapons, food, and clothing. Desertion was endemic, plus outbreaks of cholera which ravaged not only the Phalanx but also the Legitimist army and the armies of Costa Rica, Honduras, and Guatemala. However, despite leading a lackluster force, the Phalanx won the day at the Battle of Virgin Bay, where about 150 Phalanx soldiers defeated a larger Legitimist force that they cut to ribbons thanks to superior rifles. The loss at Virgin Bay caused the Legitimist army to question the competency of their commander, General Jose Santos Guardiola. What broke the army's will and resolve to fight was Walker's capture of Granada, which was accomplished thanks to Walker's use of commercial ships as both naval weapons and ferrying tools. With Granada as a bargaining chip, Walker threatened to level the town and kill Legitimist families unless the conservatives agreed to form a provisional government that included both Legitimists and Liberals.

The provisional government would not last long. The financially exhausted Nicaraguans could not stop Walker's quick takeover of the country. Because both the Legitimists and Liberals relied on conscripts, Walker's decision to end conscription in the country meant that the only standing military force left was his own. Similarly, following Walker's demand that Nicaragua hold a general election in order to name a new official government, both the Legitimists and the Liberals, the latter of whom grew disenchanted with the American following a series of summary executions of Legitimist officials and Liberal traitors, boycotted the elections. This made it a *fait accompli* that William Walker would be named as the new president of Nicaragua. This decision galvanized the conservative governments of Nicaragua's neighbors. Honduras, El Salvador, Guatemala, and Costa Rica joined forces with the remnants of Nicaragua's two armies to remove all of Walker's 850 armed men from Central America. The Central Americans rallied to the cause along racial lines, saying that Walker's intent was to supplant the mixed-race nations of Central America with a White one from the north (i.e., the US).[12] Walker did indeed see his crusade as a racial one, arguing that his army, which represented naturalized citizens of Nicaragua, had the right to rule the land not only because they had shed their blood to win it, but because generations of misuse of the land and economy by the locals required an injection of Anglo-Saxon civilization in order to set it right. The war to remove President Walker became a war of extermination, with innocent American and European merchants and farmers targeted for execution by Costa Rican soldiers.[13]

Cornelis Vanderbilt also entered the fray as the most powerful member of the anti-Walker coalition. Opposed to filibustering and incensed at Walker's expropriation of Accessory Transit Company property, Vanderbilt hired a New York ruffian and former murder suspect named Sylvanus Spencer to retake Walker's purloined ships one by one. Spencer did his job well, and his crew of 120 Costa Rican soldiers successfully destroyed Walker's ad-hoc navy while the Phalanx was fighting for its life against thousands of Central American soldiers. Without an escape route to the sea, Walker's men were forced to abandon Granada after a grueling siege where Henningsen's small squadron defended a single church in the city square for two weeks against a much larger force commanded by Salvadoran General Ramon Belloso.[14]

Fighting retreats, disease, and desertion decimated Walker's army. On May 1st, 1857, Walker and his coterie of soldiers, POWs, and armed Nicaraguan loyalists surrendered to Captain Charles H.

Davis of the US Navy. The undaunted Walker returned to New Orleans still proclaiming himself as the legitimate president of Nicaragua. He still lusted after military adventure, too. After giving lectures across New Orleans, San Francisco, and New York, Walker was approached by a representative of the Bay Islands. Located off the coast of Honduras, the Bay Islands belonged to the British Empire as part of their Mosquito Kingdom protectorate. However, in 1860, London signaled to Honduras that it wanted to give up the islands so long as Tegucigalpa agreed to respect the rights and liberties of the British citizens living on the islands. London encouraged the islanders to relocate to Jamaica or Barbados, but instead a delegate from the town of Coxen Hole asked Walker to assemble a new force to act as a line of defense against Honduras. Walker agreed.

In June 1860, Walker's expedition set off from their base at Cozumel, Mexico and planned to land at Coxen Hole. Patrolling Royal Navy ships convinced Walker to land at Trujillo on the Honduran mainland instead. There, Walker's men stormed Fortaleza de Santa Barbara and took it with a minor loss of life. Although it sent the Honduran army out of Trujillo, Walker's seizure of the fort was a pyrrhic victory. Offshore, Commander Nowell Salmon of the Royal Navy threatened to unleash his guns on the Americans. When Walker agreed to surrender to Salmon as a representative of the British crown, the Tennessee filibuster ended his final campaign. Sadly for Walker, Salmon used sub-terfuge in handing Walker and an officer over to the Hondurans. Since Walker continued to claim that he was the rightful president of Nicaragua, Commander Salmon forced Walker into Honduran custody on charges of an unlawful declaration of war against a peaceful neighbor. On September 12th, 1860, a Honduran firing squad executed the thirty-six-year-old William Walker.

Of the few people who ever recorded their personal inter-actions with Walker, all agreed that his dream was to build an English-speaking empire in Central America. As a dictator, Walker would establish an independent republic that would offer a regional alternative to both the US and the British Empire. Walker's support for slavery was multi-faceted. On the one hand it was based in *realpolitik*—Walker understood that a slave-owning Central American republic could more easily conduct trade with the South and attract Southern immigrants. Walker also believed in the superiority of Anglo-Saxon civilization, saying that the "half caste" majority of Nicaragua as well as Africans only enjoyed the "teaching of the arts of life" thanks to White Europeans. [15] Despite this contempt for Latin America and its multi-racial civilization, Walker felt strongly that he had become a citizen of Nicaragua and believed sincerely that his government had improved daily life for the average Nicaraguan. Walker even converted to Catholicism to show his commitment to his adoptive country.

One year before Walker's death, his ideal of a Southern-style republic in Central America was echoed by George Bickley, a quack Cincinnati doctor who formed the Knights of the Golden Circle after a failed filibustering expedition to Mexico. The Knights sought to create the so-called "Golden Circle," a Southern dominion of slave-owning governments in the Caribbean, Central America, and Mexico. An 1861 book penned by an anonymous member of the secret society even claimed Walker as a member.[16]

After the Civil War, thousands of Southerners sought to follow Walker's lead by relocating to Latin America as a favorable alternative to Northern tyranny. Confederate veterans established colonies like New Virginia in Mexico or Americana in Brazil. The latter still enjoys celebrating its Southern history and heritage, which saw 10,000 Southern immigrants establish Protestant churches and modern agricultural techniques in the impoverished Brazilian jungle. Frank McMullen, a veteran of Walker's war in Nicaragua, was the Texan most responsible for the Southern presence in Brazil.

Like the lion Walker, approximately 5,000 Southerners, many of whom were fresh from Civil War battlefields like General John B. Magruder, pledged loyalty to Emperor Maximilian of Mexico and fought bravely for his empire. A similar Confederate veteran was an ancestor of this writer, who went from mercenary service in Mexico to a generalship in the army of the Khedive of Egypt.

All these men were imbued with the spirit of William Walker— America's very own *conquistador*. Given that as recently as 2018, some Bay Islanders petitioned to return to the British

Commonwealth, maybe Walker's dream isn't dead but waiting for a figurehead with the courage and gall to carve out a private kingdom.

[1] Scott Martelle, *William Walker's Wars: How One Man's Private American Army Tried to Conquer Mexico, Nicaragua, and Honduras* (Chicago: Chicago Review Press, 2019): 20.
[2] Stephen Kinzer, "Nicaragua: The Beleaguered Revolution," *New York Times Magazine*, 28 Aug. 1983, https://www.nytimes.com/1983/08/28/magazine/nicaragua-the-beleaguered-revolution.html.
[3] Martelle, *William Walker's Wars*, 201.
[4] Ibid., 9.
[5] Ibid., 17.
[6] Ibid., 34.
[7] Ibid., 67.
[8] Ibid., 86.
[9] Benjamin Welton, "Uncle Sam's Intervention," *Military History*, January 2020.
[10] Martelle, *William Walker's Wars*, 119.
[11] Ibid., 203.
[12] Ibid., 185.
[13] Ibid., 186.
[14] Ibid., 209–210.
[15] Ibid., 200.
[16] *An Authentic Exposition of the "K.G.C." or, A History of Secession from 1834 to 1861* (Indianapolis: C.O. Perrine): 186

American "isolationism" never really existed. The myth of isolationism often obscures the US Navy's long history of small-scale expeditions done in the name of commerce and civilization. However, an older America had a much saner and more limited foreign policy—a foreign policy based around protecting the Western Hemisphere and keeping the shipping lanes open. A foreign policy like this, which privileges the Navy over the Army, could easily return America to its lost greatness.[1]

One of the other great myths of the modern world is that America is not and has never been at war with Islam. Any serious student of history can spy the deep-seated lie almost immediately. The West, which used to be just called Christendom, has been in conflict with the Prophet Muhammad since his religion stormed out of the Arabian deserts in the seventh century. Few students today know or care that the Middle East and North Africa that the Islamic hordes conquered was culturally Roman, ethnically Berber and Levantine, and religiously Christian.[2] Of course, it also goes without saying that the Umayyad conquest of Spain was an act of cultural destruction that forever cut the advanced Hispano-Visigoths from history. Rather than bring with them Aristotle or the genius of Indian or Persian mathematics, the Islamic invaders stopped a Christian and Romanized culture from reaching its full potential. The Berber-Arab invaders knew that they had defeated a superior civilization. Recognizing this, many if not most of the Islamic rulers of Spain were the fair-haired offspring of Christian slave women.[3]

Centuries later, Islam had not changed much. The new Islamic power, Ottoman Turkey, had twice threatened Western Europe at the gates of Vienna before being repulsed by a Christian coalition. By the earl nineteenth century, the Ottoman Empire was clearly in decline. However, thanks to their ports in North Africa and their territories in the Balkans and East Africa, Constantinople (the Turkish capital did not become Istanbul until the twentieth century) continued on with its lucrative slave trade without much in the way of interference.[4]

Enter a new power—the secular and liberal United States of America. Influenced by the Enlightenment and the Anglo-Scottish championing of capitalist enterprise, Washington, D.C. quickly began a campaign of international trade. This provided the centerpiece for early American foreign policy, and the small US Navy became the chief disseminator of America economic power abroad. Unfortunately, unlike the British Royal Navy, the fledging American Navy could not fully guarantee the safety of US citizens involved in the Mediterranean Sea trade. Such a limitation proved fatal due to the Ottoman policy of state-sponsored piracy.

Realizing the weakness of the new Atlantic power, the independent Sultanate of Morocco and the Ottoman Beylik of Tunis, Eyalet of Tripolitania, and the Regency of Algiers stepped up their campaign of raiding merchant ships and taking crews hostage. Many of these sailors became slaves for the "Sublime Porte." Realizing that American commerce would be adversely affected by continuous piracy, Presidents Thomas Jefferson and James Madison decided to act with force.

The most famous event of both the First and Second Barbary Wars was the burning of the USS *Philadelphia* in February 1804. Five months earlier, Ottoman pirates had seized the frigate after it ran aground just outside of Tripoli's main harbor. At the time, Commodore Edward Preble was launching constant naval attacks on the Barbary corsairs and was close to winning the war. However, when 307 American sailors fell into Barbary hands, Preble's light at the end of the tunnel dimmed.

Convinced that the *Philadelphia* had to be destroyed. Lieutenant Stephen Decatur, Jr. volunteered for the dangerous mission. After nightfall on February 16th, 1804, Decatur's ship the *Intrepid* crept into Tripoli's harbor. Decatur's men dressed up like Maltese and Arab pirates and boarded the *Philadelphia*. Without losing a single man, the Intrepid's raiding party managed to free the American hostages and kill about twenty Tripolitan pirates.[5]

While the war would drag on, and the USS *Constitution* (which remains in active service today) was called upon to win the Second Battle of Tripoli Harbor, Decatur's daring raid effectively took the starch out of the Muslim corsairs.

Many historians, especially those trained in the Marxist style of complete materialism, consider the Barbary Wars nothing more than a commerce conflict. It is believed that America was inspired by economics, not religion or even national pride. However, President Thomas Jefferson knew full well that the Barbary pirates were animated by Islam more than the desire for wealth. In 1785, Jefferson and John Adams met Tripoli's ambassador in London. During their chat, the American delegation broached the subject of Islamic piracy. Namely, they wanted to know why the men of North Africa felt justified in taking American and British ships. "It was written in the Koran," the ambassador told them, "that all Nations who should not have acknowledged their [Muslim] authority were sinners, that it was their right and duty to make war upon whoever they could find and to make Slaves of all they could take as prisoners, and that every Mussulman who should be slain in battle was sure to go to Paradise."[6]

Such disdain for non-believers was repeated again later in the 1830s when the US Navy was called in to deal with another set of Islamic pirates. This time the battleground was in Asia, specifically the Dutch East Indies (today's Indonesia). Erroneously considered a bastion of "progressive" or at least "tolerant" Islam, Indonesia, then as now, belonged to Sunni Islamists.[7] Prior to the two expeditions to Sumatra, American merchants, especially those based in Salem, Massachusetts, had a flourishing relationship with the Aceh Sultanate, one of the world's greatest exporters of pepper. In February 1831, the vessel *Friendship*, which was owned by the wealthy Salem shipbuilder Joseph Peabody, was attacked by local pirates who killed the ship's first officer and two crew members. Yet another hostage situation developed.

Fortunately for the crew of the *Friendship*, three US ships—the *Palmer*, the *James Monroe*, and the *Governor Endicott*—were armed and in the area. Their appearance scared off the pirates and the *Friendship* ultimately made it back to Salem.

An outraged President Andrew Jackson decided that such villainy could not stand. He ordered Commodore John Downes to redirect his ship from Brazil to Kuala Batee, the location of the *Friendship*'s ordeal. On February 6th, 1832, the *Potomac*, which had been disguised as a Dutch merchant vessel, attacked Kuala Batee with a sustained bombardment and the deployment of some 282 Marines.[8] About 100 Sumatrans died in the battle, while the area's defenses lay in ruins. A similarly punitive expedition was carried out between December 1838 and January 1839 after Muslim Malay pirates of the Aceh Sultanate once again attacked another American merchant vessel.

While some have characterized these sea-based battles as early skirmishes in the long War on Terror, the truth is that the US's first sustained contact with Islamic fighters did not occur until 1901. At that time, the US had already become an imperial power, with Puerto Rico, Guam, the Panama Canal, and the Philippines all under direct US control. The relative ease of the Spanish-American War gave way to the brutish jungle fighting of the Philippine-American War of 1899. Until 1902, US soldiers fought a Filipino insurgency that utilized guerrilla tactics that eerily presaged the Vietminh and the Vietcong. Unlike the later Indochina War, the US military successfully pacified the Philippines, but at a terrible cost. Over 6,000 Americans were killed, while approximately 20,000 Filipinos died. The US also practiced the "water cure," a type of early waterboarding, in order to break the will of the guerrillas.

Even before the larger war could be resolved, a second front opened on the Muslim majority island of Mindanao. Here, Moro rebels, whom the Spanish called "Moros" because they reminded them of their old Moorish enemies from Morocco, Tunis, and Algiers, took up arms against their new masters. American military leaders feared that the Moros, who practiced polygamy and the use of "infidel" slaves, would treat the American troops like they did the Spanish by capturing lone grunts, torturing them for hours in the jungle, emasculating them, and burning them alive.[9]

The fearsome Moro tribesmen utilized suicide attacks made by *amok*s, berserker-like Muslim warriors. Such people proved unwilling to be "civilized" by President William McKinley and President Theodore Roosevelt. The notion of American civilization and attendant Protestant Christianity was anathema to the Moros and the people of the Sulu Archipelago. They saw no reason to change their traditional habits of pillaging, internecine warfare, piracy, and slave-taking.

Therefore, not long after US Marines landed at Zamboanga, members of the Moro Maranaos tribe began attacking American jungle camps. By 1902, *Juramentados*, or Muslim warriors who had sworn an oath to attack all opponents of Islam, began harassing US military patrols all over Mindanao. The *Juramentados* were feared for their bravery and zealotry. One of their number even managed to take several revolver rounds before he successfully chopped off an American officer's legs. (The ineffectiveness of the standard issue .38 Long Colt against Moro warriors led to the adoption of the .45 ACP round by the US military.)

Ultimately, a new military commander, the old Indian fighter Captain John J. Pershing, found the right formula against the Moros. Believing that the Muslim warriors only respected force, Pershing pursued a hammer-fisted policy against the rebels. At every opportunity, American forces used artillery to bombard Moro *cotas*, or wood and bamboo forts, before mopping up all resistance with infantry charges. "Civilize 'em with the Krag" became the motto of Pershing's men.

Pershing's successor, Major General Leonard Wood, continued the program of aggressive jungle probes combined with attempts to integrate his men with the local Moro communities. As the military governor of Mindanao, Wood faced multiple tribal rebellions that resulted in over 100 expeditions to Jolo and beyond. Wood's biggest moment in the Philippines came when his forces climbed 2,000 feet in order to take on 600 Moros hunkered down in the extinct volcano at Bud Dajo. Although the American press would characterize this battle as too savage, Wood won the day.

Until 1913, when between 6,000 and 10,000 Moro warriors made their last stand against the Americans at Bud Bagsak, the Moro Rebellion stayed as nothing more than low-level insurgency. America's ultimate victory there proved fleeting. Today, under the rule of Manila, Mindanao and the majority Muslim provinces of the south continue to bedevil the Philippine security forces, who often rely on American military aid. As was the case in Tripoli, Sumatra, and Jolo City, Islam remains the animating force of the opposition. The deadly siege of Marawi in 2017, which displaced 120,000 after the ISIS-linked Maute Group briefly captured the city,[10] is the most vicious and visceral example of Islam's power within the *Pax Americana*.

---

[1] Michael Anton, "America and the Liberal International Order," *American Affairs*, Vol. I, No. I (Spring 2017): 113–125.

[2] Alistair Boddy-Evans, "Early Christianity in North Africa," *Thought Co*, Feb. 17, 2019, https://www.thoughtco.com/early-christianity-in-north-africa-part-1-444 61.

[3] Dario Fernandez-Morera, *The Myth of the Andalusian Paradise: Muslims, Christians, and Jews under Islamic Rule in Medieval Spain* (Wilmington, DE: ISI Books, 2016).

[4] "The White Salves of Barbary North Africa and the Ottoman Empire," *Renegade Tribune*, Sept. 1, 2015, http://www.renegadetribune.com/the-white-slaves-of-barbary-north-africa-and-the-ottoman-empire/?doing_wp_cron=1609198155.71 86539173126220703125.

[5] Julius Melero, "The Burning of the USS *Philadelphia*," *Naval History Blog*, Feb. 18, 2015, https://www.navalhistory.org/2015/02/18/the-burning-of-the-uss-philadelphia.

[6] Christopher Hitchens, "Jefferson Versus the Muslim Pirates," *City Journal*, Spring 2007.

[7] Jacobus E. Lato, "Indonesia: U.S. vs. Reality," *Gatestone Institute*, May 16, 2017, https://www.gatestoneinstitute.org/10355/indonesia-pence-visit.

[8] Antoine Vanner, "The US Navy's Sumatran Expeditions 1832 & 1838," *Duty and Daring in the Heyday of Empire*, Jan. 26, 2016, http://dawlishchronicles. blogspot.com/2016/01/the-us-navys-sumatran-expeditions-1832.html.

[9] David S. Woolman, "Fighting Islam's Fierce Moro Warriors - America's first war with suicidal Islamic warriors," *Military History Magazine*, April 2002.

[10] Ashley Westerman, "Over 120,000 People Remain Displaced 3 Years After Philippines' Marawi Battle," *NPR.org*, Oct. 23, 2020, https://www.npr.org/2020 /10/23/925316298/over-120-000-people-remain-displaced-3-years-after-philippines-marawi-battleThe.

ISLAMIC STATE IN THE VICTORIAN ERA

American Renaissance, March 29th, 2019.

We've fought with many men acrost the seas,
An' some of 'em was brave an' some was not:
The Paythan an' the Zulu an' Burmese;
But the Fuzzy was the finest o' the lot.
We never got a ha'porth's change of 'im:
'E squatted in the scrub an' 'ocked our 'orses,
'E cut our sentries up at Sua~kim~,
An' 'e played the cat an' banjo with our forces.
So 'ere's ~to~ you, Fuzzy-Wuzzy, at your 'ome in the Soudan;
You're a pore benighted 'eathen but a first-class fightin' man;
                    —"Fuzzy-Wuzzy," Rudyard Kipling (1892)

Rudyard Kipling, the great bard of British imperialism, echoed the sentiment of many British fighting men in his poem "Fuzzy-Wuzzy." But who were the Fuzzy-Wuzzy who "was the finest o' the lot" when it came to the enemies of the British Army? The answer: the Beja tribesmen of Sudan. Renowned for their pastoralism, fierce independence, and their elaborate and wild-looking hairstyles, the Beja and other Sudanese tribes battled the Anglo-Egyptian army between 1883 and 1899. During that protracted war, the fearless Beja frequently rode hard and fast directly into the teeth of British military steel armed only with spears and small swords. The reason? The Beja scorned men who used firearms, plus, during the late nineteenth century, the Beja pledged their loyalty to Mohammed Ahmed, the professed Mahdi of Islam.

In Michael Asher's excellent book, *Khartoum: The Ultimate Imperial Adventure*, the Beja, specifically the "ethnically pure" Amarar, claim descent from Noah's son Ham and may be related to "the same pre-dynastic stock from which the ancestors of the pharaohs had sprung."[1] While recent genetic testing calls this assertion into question, there is no doubt that the Beja are an ancient people with a long tradition of rugged liberty. In 1880 or 1881, the Beja and other Sudanese tribes rallied around a humble worker with little religious teaching. That worker was Mohammed Ahmed, who had been proclaimed as the savior of Islam (*Mahdi*) by a wandering holy man (*feki*) from Darfur named Abdallahi wad Torshayn.[2] Neither Ahmad nor Abdallahi came from one of the powerful tribes of the Sudan, with Ahmed being a Danagla and Abdallahi belonging to the hated Ta'isha clan of the Baggara nomads.[3] Despite this handicap, the declaration of the Mahdi drew thousands of Sudanese to Ahmed, and from there he and his inner circle began demanding a purification of their lands and a return to the "pure" Islam of the seventh century.

The first target of Mahdist rage was the ruling Turco-Egyptian elite. Venal and corrupt, Ottoman officials in the Sudan had few friends among the Sudanese or the British. For the dervishes (the Western name for Mahdist soldiers), the Turco-Egyptian bureaucrats were apostates—Sunni Muslims who did not truly practice or appreciate the faith. Even worse, many non-Muslims, including Jews and Greek, Assyrian, and Armenian Christians, could be found in the Ottoman civil service.

Unfortunately, for the Khedive of Egypt, Tewfik, his government could not just let Sudan rot. Tewfik's ancestor, the great Muhammad Ali, had conquered much of the Sudan in 1822. Since then, the Sudan was a colony of a colony (Egypt remained a nominal province of the Ottoman Empire until the late nineteenth century), and despite the fact that Sudan was not an economic engine or vitally important to protecting Egypt's southern border, Cairo felt the need to maintain its hegemony south of the Sahara. Therefore, in 1883, Tewfik sent an expeditionary force into the Sudan to put down the Muslim insurgency.

The expedition that reached the Sudan in that year included 8,300 infantrymen, 2,000 cavalry troops, sixteen Krupp mountain-guns, and numerous Nordenfeldt machine-guns.[4] This modern force was led by a cadre of European officers, including Major Baron Gotz von Seckendorff of Prussia, Major Arthur

Herlth of Austria-Hungary, and Valentine Baker, a former officer of Britain's 10th Hussars who had been forced to leave the service following a sex scandal. The overall commander was William Hicks, aka Hicks Pasha. A veteran of the British East India Company's Bombay Army, Hicks had cut his teeth during the genocidal fighting in the Sepoy Mutiny of 1857. Between 1867 and 1868, Hicks had been a general during Britain's Abyssinian Expedition, which successfully punished Emperor Tewodros II of Ethiopia for imprisoning European missionaries. Hicks was one of many European military men lured to Egypt with promises of wealth and status as members of the modernizing army.

Despite great equipment and capable generals, the expeditionary of 1883 was nothing more than a paper tiger. Most of the men in Hicks's army had been conscripted into service, and these Egyptian peasants (*fellahin*) were known to mutilate themselves to avoid serving in the Sudan. Unsurprisingly, when Mohammed Ahmed's 40,000 dervishes ambushed Hicks's force at El Obeid in November 1883, thousands of Egyptian soldiers dropped their weapons and fled. Others begged for their lives and hoped that their Muslim faith would spare them from a gruesome death. Many of these men would be stripped naked and sold as slaves in Mahdist markets.

As for Hicks and the Europeans, history records that they went down fighting. Gustav Klootz, the German socialist and deserter who betrayed Hicks's men to the dervishes, said years later that Hicks and the other Europeans killed several enemies before finally dying themselves. Sheikh Ali Gulla, a dervish veteran of the battle, claimed that Hicks "was full of courage like an elephant."[5] The British general apparently emptied and reloaded his revolver three times, then, after exhausting his last bullets, Hicks charged into the middle of a dervish column and fought them with his sword. Hicks's heroics, along with the bravery of the other White officers, impressed the Beja warriors but did not stop them from mutilating Hicks and Seckendorff after their deaths.

The news of the Hicks Expedition's slaughter triggered a panic in Cairo. British military and civilian leaders, who had wielded the only real authority in the country since 1882, were conflicted over what to do about the Mahdist revolt. Sir Evelyn Baring (the future

Lord Cromer) thought that Sudan should go to the dogs. After all, Egypt's economy was still in shambles, and Sir Evelyn thought that it was in Britain's interest to clean up Cairo's coffers before undertaking any kind of punitive expedition. This sentiment was, for a time, echoed by Lieutenant General Lord Garnet Wolseley, the very same man who had won Egypt in the first place.

On the other side of the equation stood several British Army officers and politicians, especially those in the Conservative Party who saw the collapse of Anglo-Egyptian power in the Sudan as indicative of the weak rule of Liberal Prime Minister William Ewart Gladstone. In 1884, owing to pressure from the general public and Queen Victoria herself, Gladstone's government decided to send a military envoy to the Sudan to observe and report on the situation. The man they chose would become one of the Victorian era's great martyrs.

Major General Charles "Chinese" Gordon was an intellectual, a devout Christian, a mystic, and a wonderful field commander. Gordon had earned the nickname "Chinese" in the 1860s when he had served as one of the European commanders of Qing China's Ever Victorious Army. Paid for by European and American merchants living in Shanghai, Hong Kong, and other port cities, and commanded by a colorful cast of mercenaries and experienced military veterans, the Ever Victorious Army played a role in ending the bloody Taiping Rebellion. The clear-eyed Gordon would go on to remark that the average Chinese soldier "fought for loot only" and would run away most of the time.[6] Gordon, who had previously served as the Governor-General of the Sudan, held a similarly dismal view of the average Sudanese trooper.

Not long after establishing himself as the new British viceroy in Khartoum (which the Gladstone government had explicitly forbidden), Gordon and his garrison found themselves under siege from a dervish force numbering over 50,000 men. Gordon, who could only rely on 7,000 Egyptian and Sudanese troops, sent back several reports to Cairo and London warning them of the ugly situation. Many of these reports were ignored, while most were received many weeks after they had been sent. Thus, Gordon and his starving garrison had to wait for months until a relief expedition was even discussed, let alone assembled.

General Wolseley, an ardent supporter of Gordon, assembled the Gordon Relief Expedition in late 1884. Rather than make the same mistake as Hicks, Wolseley and his hand-picked officers went south with a mostly British force. Several crack regiments partook in the expedition, including the Royal Marines, 1st Battalion, Black Watch, the Gordon Highlanders, the 19th Hussars, and the York & Lancaster Regiment. Wolseley also created one of the first modern special forces units, the Desert Column, and staffed it with Britain's best cavalry soldiers and put them on Arab camels. Like the Victorian army generally, the vast majority of the soldiers who fought in the Nile Campaign were Englishmen.[7]

These British troops would fight several gory battles with the "Fuzzy-Wuzzy" in the Sudan between 1884 and 1885. At the Battle of et-Teb, the British suffered thirty-five casualties, while their dervish opponents lost over 2,000 men.[8] During that same battle, when the Royal Navy's *Hecla* fell under attack, Captain Arthur Wilson fended off Beja spearmen with his sword. Despite being stabbed in the abdomen, Wilson managed to decapitate and otherwise kill several enemies. At one point, after his sword broke, Wilson fought with just his fists.

Other outsized examples of British manliness included the actions of Colonel Fred Burnaby, who went to the Sudan as a civilian armed only with a double-barreled shotgun. At et-Teb, Burnaby managed to fire twenty-three shells that killed a total of thirteen dervish warriors.[9] At the later Battle of Tamaai, the legendary Black Watch launched an impromptu bayonet charge when their fighting square was breached. The average British soldier proved in 1884–1885 that they were better than the "Fuzzy-Wuzzy" at their own game, namely frontal charges conducted with only cold steel.

Sadly, the Nile Expedition failed in its main objective. On January 26th, 1885, thousands of Mahdist troops stormed into Khartoum and took the city. Gordon, like fellow British lion Hicks, fought to his last gasp. According to his aide-de-camp, Gordon retreated to his palace armed with a revolver and a sword. For an untold number of minutes, Gordon fired and reloaded his revolver, while also hacking and slashing dervish spearmen. Gordon killed and wounded an untold number of Sudanese tribesmen before his death due to a combination of multiple stab wounds and at least one revolver bullet in his chest. Like Hicks, Gordon's body was defiled and decapitated. For the rest of her life, Queen Victoria would blame the slow-moving Gladstone for Gordon's death.[10]

Gordon's martyrdom became well-known throughout the British Empire. Fewer knew about happened to the small European population in Khartoum after the dervish takeover. Nikolaos Leontides, the city's Greek consul, had his hands severed before his head. An entire Greek family was destroyed—the father shot in the head, the son brained with an ax, and the pregnant wife taken as a concubine for a dervish harem. Martin Hansall, the Austro-Hungarian consul, had his head lopped off when a former servant betrayed him to a group of spearmen. Franz Klein, a tailor and a Catholic convert of Hungarian Jewish heritage, had his throat slit. His Italian wife and their five children were forced to watch, then one of them (a daughter) was raped by the killers. The city's Catholic Mission was likewise raided and left drenched in blood.[11]

The people of Britain would have to wait until 1896 to have their revenge. In the meantime, the Sudan became a theocratic state controlled by religious fanatics. Mahdist Sudan prefigured the Islamic State by more than a hundred years, and Mahdist policy likewise encouraged rape and the entire cleansing of tribes suspected of being loyal to the Anglo-Egyptian government. This nightmare only ended in 1898 at the Battle of Omdurman. Here, a British, Egyptian, and Sudanese army of over 25,000 men utterly decimated a dervish force numbering 52,000. The British, who utilized Maxim machine guns and the latest in artillery and rifles, suffered less than fifty dead. The Mahdists lost about 12,000. A year later, the entire Sudan was pacified.

The British would leave the Sudan for good in 1955. Looking at the current state of Great Britain today, it is hard to believe that it once produced the world's best soldiers and sailors. British men stood steady at the four corners of the world. In the Sudan, the same spirit of Rorke's Drift prevailed, for the British were almost always outnumbered by their opponents. They may have re-spected the Beja, but every British soldier and imperial adventurer knew that Anglo-Saxon vigor would always win the day.

As for the dervish warriors, their bravery became legendary, but so too did their cruelty. The men who fought for Sudan's Islamic state presaged not only the callous fighters of ISIS, but also the drug-fueled Simba Communists, who, in 1964, raped, tortured, and murdered the White residents of Stanleyville before a combined Belgian and mercenary relief force could save the day. Echoes of the dervish menace linger in Sudan and South Sudan today, for both nations are plagued by wandering gunmen who use rape as a political tool.

Thanks to our vicious elites Sudan's old problems are now our new problems. British, Ottoman, and Egyptian officials learned to deal the bloodlust and sexual appetites of Sudanese tribesmen. We have to learn to deal with it now ourselves.

---

[1] Asher, Michael. *Khartoum: The Ultimate Imperial Adventure* (London: Penguin, 2006): 28.
[2] Asher, *Khartoum*, 51.
[3] Ibid., 47.
[4] Ibid., xxiii.
[5] Ibid., xxii.
[6] Ibid., 72.
[7] Ibid., 111.
[8] Raugh, Harold E. *The Victorians At War, 1815–1914: An Encyclopedia of British Military History* (Santa Barbara: ABC-CLIO, 2004): 132.
[9] Asher, *Khartoum*, 121.
[10] Ibid., 280
[11] Ibid., 261–262

A SOUTH AFRICAN TRAGEDY

American Renaissance, May 23rd, 2019.

The Boer War
By Martin Bossenbroek
Seven Stories Press, 2018
464 Pages

From the perspective of 2018, it is hard to see the Second Anglo-Boer War (1899–1902) as anything other than a tragedy. One could even call it "White-on-White crime." The war saw a force of 60,000 South African Boer militiamen (*commandos*) wage war with the world's greatest military power, the British Empire. At first, the tough and ready Boers of the Transvaal and the Orange Free State managed to push into the Natal Colony, where some 16,000-plus British troops waited for them. The initial success of the Boers was nothing short of a bloody nose to the British officer corps. These haughty men, many of whom earned their spurs fighting the Pathans in the Northwest Frontier or Muslim fanatics in Sudan, considered the Boers nothing more than uncouth, antediluvian Dutch Protestants who could not defeat the professional British Army in any contest. They were proven wrong early in the conflict.

Such arrogance was, to put it mildly, not based in real and recent history. Between 1880 and 1881, the South African Republic (Transvaal) defeated the British Army and its Natal and Transvaal colonies. Following the First Anglo-Boer War, the Boers earned the right to rule their own republics without interference from Cape Town (the British base of operations in their part of South Africa) or London. The ardent imperialists of Britain saw things rather differently.

As recounted in Dutch historian Martin Bossenbroek's book *The Boer War*, the events of 1899 truly began a decade earlier when gold was found in the Transvaal. Almost overnight the city of Johannesburg sprang into life. This bustling metropolis was a boom town right out of the American Wild West—bordellos, gambling saloons, and all types of vices were bought and sold in this city. President Paul Kruger of the Transvaal, who was affectionately known as "Oom Paul" ("Uncle Paul") by his fellow Boers, despised Johannesburg and the men who were drawn to it with every fiber of his being. Kruger, Bossenbroek writes, epitomized the Old Testament zeal of a veld-bred farmer and cattle rustler who came from the proud *Voortrekker* stock that soundly thrashed the mighty Zulus at the Battle of Blood River.

For "Oom Paul" and others, Johannesburg and the gold rush in the Transvaal remind them too much of what they had seen back in the Cape Colony. Previously, the Eastern Cape had been the Boer's land—a gorgeous stretch of beach and farmable soil where liberty-loving Boers (a heterogeneous mix of White South Africans of Dutch, Huguenot, German, Spanish, and Portuguese descent) lived in a manner not unlike the one seen in the Massachusetts Bay Colony. However, by the early nineteenth century, the British called the Cape a "protectorate" and quickly turned that part of South Africa into a colony. The Afrikaans-speaking Boers who wanted nothing to do with British rule moved eastward into the high veld. There they met and defeated several Black African tribes, thus establishing to the two republics that Britain sought to quash in 1899.

The Boer War is a wonderful throwback to the days of heroic (which essentially means of Indo-European) history. First published in Dutch in 2012 and only recently translated into English, *The Boer War* essentially divides the story into three. The war part of the story, with its tales of battle, commando raids, and guerrilla warfare, takes as its primary star the former British Army officer and war correspondent Winston Churchill. For fans of Candace Millard's excellent book *Hero of the Empire*, this chunk of the book is familiar territory. That being said, Bossenbroek does provide a lot of insightful details about the divisions within the British Army in 1899 (the "Indian" vs "African" officers) as well as the divisions within the Boer camp. The book's first and most boring section prominently features Willem Leyds, a young Dutch lawyer who is hired by the South African Republic not long after graduation. This section is dominated by tales of South African politics and economic transactions between the Boers, the French, the Germans, and the Portuguese colony of Mozambique. But even here some big personalities steal the show. Chief among them is Cecil Rhodes, the brilliant mining magnate who took a band of handpicked mercenaries across the Limpopo River and established the British state of Rhodesia. Not to be outdone, Rhodes envisioned all of South Africa as a British confederation. The combative Boers stood in the way of this Cape-to-Cairo vision.

Bossenbroek's final section deals with Deneys Reitz, the brave Boer commando leader who wound up exiled to Madagascar following the Boer defeat. Here, Reitz's own memoir of the war, entitled *Commando: A Boer Journal of the Boer War*, provides the source material for Bossenbroek's description of the war's bloody guerrilla phase. At this point, when the British could not decisively defeat the highly mobile and well-armed Boers, they resorted to placing Boer women and children in concentration camps. These filthy, disease-ridden camps became the great scandal of the early twentieth century, with British and European journalists penning outraged articles about the horrendous suffering of White infants and their mothers and grandmothers. Today, it is believed that somewhere around 26,000 people died in these camps due to starvation and disease. Incredibly, despite this heinous deed, Reitz and several other Boers fought alongside the British and the Union of South Africa during World War I against the German Empire.

For dissidents in America, there is much to digest and learn from *The Boer War*. First of all, for Americans, Canadians, Australians, and New Zealanders, it is much easier to identify with the Boers than it is with the White ethnics of Europe. Unlike, say, the English or the Germans, the native Whites of North America are an ethnic hodgepodge historically united by their Christian faith and shared experiences in the American wilderness. This accurately describes the Boer experience and the Rhodesian experience as well. The Boers of 1899 mostly wanted to be left alone in their republics. Millions of Americans feel the same way today.

One of the key reasons why Britain felt the need to get involved in Boer affairs was because of the *Uitlanders*. This Afrikaans term denoted all those non-Boer immigrants who rushed into the Transvaal in order to make easy money. A majority of these immigrants were British citizens, and by the late 1890s, they made up a majority of the population in the urban Transvaal. Before long, these economic immigrants demanded voting rights and equal protection under the law. The South African Republic was willing to bargain but resisted the idea of giving the *Uitlanders* the same footing as the native Boer in their own ethnic states. Unsatisfied, the *Uitlanders* organized their own political action committees and even tried sabotage. The Jameson Raid of 1895 failed to stir up the expected rebellion of Brits in the Transvaal, but it did prove to the Boers that Britain was serious about putting its own people first.

For us in the twenty-first century, the parallels are clear. Today in the United States, the government of Mexico profits from the exportation of its cheap labor while simultaneously agitating for anti-White, pro-Hispanic causes. Mexico City does not even try to hide its motivations, and groups like La Raza make it abundantly clear that they see illegal immigration as the Great War strategy for the *Reconquista*. In Victorian South Africa and present-day America, demographics is destiny.

Also like the British of the nineteenth century, today's race warriors often hide their intentions behind masks of charity. The Boers countered British propaganda by exposing London, especially its Christian missionaries, as infatuated with the myth of the "noble savage." British do-gooders often chastised the Boers for failing to live up to the civilizing mission of White Christians in Africa, and many accused the Boers of outright racial hostility to their Black and colored neighbors. The Boers were under no such illusions about their neighbors; they had been fighting against vengeful tribes all of their lives, and unlike the "redneck" British, the Boers actually knew how to make peace with African tribes. Such cultural ignorance would be repeated during the Apartheid era, when left-wing British governments and their allies successfully harassed, boycotted, and harangued the Boers into giving Blacks the right to vote in elections. Since then, South Africa has spiraled into chaos, with the "rainbow nation" that once promised racial harmony giving way to endemic corruption, rape, and murder. Unsurprisingly, the targets of most racial attacks in South Africa are Whites, both Anglo and Boer. This reality would not have surprised the frontline commandos of 1900, nor would it have surprised the Cold War commando Mike Hoare, the Anglo-Irish South African transplant who told journalist Hans Germani that left-wing politics in Africa is "a fanatic movement against the White man, an appeal to wild dreams of a colored dominion of the world."[1]

Despite its horror, *The Boer War* makes it abundantly clear that it was fought during an age of true manliness. Readers of Bossnebroek's book cannot help but be dazzled by the audacity and courage of the British and Boer combatants. This was the age of hardy adventurers and Renaissance men who wrote, fought, and politicked. It is such a shame that the great British Empire that conquered Africa and India, established Singapore and Hong Kong, and helped defeat the awesome German armies of the First and Second World War felt obligated to fight the tiny, but resolute republics of the Boers. These two people should have never fought, and let the Boer War be a lesson to us that European brotherhood and the continuation of Western civilization is far more important than any temporary conflicts or disagreements.

---

[1] Germani, Hans, *White Soldiers in Black Africa: Related from His Own Experiences* (Beperk: Nasionale Boekhandel, 1967): 57.

American Renaissance, December 29th, 2017.

"Kill the foreigners and the mandarin beasts. There will be no hope for the common people until the foreigners and mandarins are gone."
—Battle Cry of the "Boxers"

In their native China, they are known as the *Yihequan*, or the Fists of Harmony and Justice. In the West, they are known as "Boxers." The name comes from their penchant for practicing Chinese martial arts and other rituals that supposedly made them impervious to bullets. Although laughable, these suicidally-brave fighters laid siege to Peking (Beijing) and Tientsin (Tianjin) for over a month, while a loose coalition of European, Japanese, and American troops scrambled to try and save their citizens from a fate worse than death. The coalition proved successful, but the Boxer Rebellion, which began as an anti-White and nationalist movement, played a large role in priming East Asia for a global confrontation. Even worse, Communist Chinese leaders have invoked the Boxers at home and abroad in order play into their genocidal designs.

Although he is a loathsome neocon who believes that Donald Trump is a Russian spook for not salivating over the idea of regime change in the Middle East, Max Boot makes several key points about the Boxer Rebellion in his book *The Savage Wars of Peace.* First and foremost, Boot argues that the Boxer Rebellion "resembled other millennial movements elsewhere . . . among peoples whose traditional way of life was crumbling before the onslaught of modernity."[1] In this case "modernity" is synonymous with Western civilization, which is itself synonymous with

European people and their progeny. It is telling that Boot compares the Boxers to the Mahdists of Sudan and the Sioux Ghost Dancers of the American West.

In the 1880s, Sudanese Muslims revolted against their Egyptian overlords. The reasons for this rebellion were multifaceted, but the chief complaint among the dark-skinned Sudanese was that lighter-skinned Arabs kept stealing their cattle and taking their relatives as slaves. A Dongolaw-speaking Nubian named Muhammad Ahmed claimed to be the "Mahdi," or messiah, and vowed to lead his people against the Ottoman- and British-backed Egyptians. The Mahdists called not only faithful Muslims to their cause, but also Arab nationalists who chafed under British suzerainty. In 1882, a large British force lead by Garnet Wolseley landed near the Suez Canal to bring order to Egypt and Sudan. Fierce fighting occurred, with Arab soldiers conducting murderous rampages all throughout Alexandria's European Quarter. US Marine officer Littleton "Tony" Waller, who led a relief force of some 132 Marines in Egypt, would recall years later seeing frenzied Arab troops murdering captured soldiers from British Indian Army units and trying to set Greek nurses on fire. According to *Honor in the Dust* author Gregg Jones, Waller would later use these experiences in Egypt to justify his harsh treatment of native insurgents during America's bloody conquest of the Philippines.

The Mahdist rebellion ended only after several Anglo-Egyptian military expeditions. It all culminated at the very lopsided Battle of Omdurman in 1898. In between 1882 and 1898, the Mahdists made a martyr out of British General Charles "Chinese" Gordon, who suffered a decapitation and post-mortem mutilation after a Mahdist army defeated his small garrison at Khartoum in 1885. Across the Atlantic, the American Army was engaged in a war with the religious fanatics of the Ghost Dance movement. Like the Mahdists, the Ghost Dance warriors were led by a prophet who promised them eternal salvation from the White man's civilization. Jack Wilson, better known as Wovoka, told his followers that the Ghost Dance ritual could drive away the White man with genocidal magic. Much like the British in Sudan, the Americans had to rely on force of arms to secure the West against the Ghost

Dance and its adherents.

The Boxer Rebellion did not happen in a vacuum, and indeed the Boxers can be seen as the Chinese equivalent of the Mahdists and Ghost Dancers (one key difference being that the Boxers did not have a central leader). However, the anti-European sentiment of the Boxers was almost exclusively based on conditions present in northern China. Ever since the two Opium Wars of the mid-nineteenth century, China had been carved up by several European powers, primarily the British and French. While the ethnically Manchu Qing dynasty remained in ostensible control, and while no parts of China were ever made into outright colonies, the concessions and spheres of influence all across coastal China made it clear that Europeans dominated Chinese trade and industry. This fact, along with a series of droughts and floods that lasted between 1898 and 1899, helped many Chinese peasants in the north to gravitate towards the Boxer movement.

As noted in Diana Preston's *The Boxer Rebellion*, the secret group had its origins in various anti-Manchu movements that sought to replace the Tungusic Manchu with a Han royal family. But, as northern China descended into greater and greater anarchy, the anti-Manchu societies began blaming the "White devils" rather than the Qing for their misfortunes. By 1898, the primary Boxer slogan was "Support the Manchus, Destroy the Foreign." Boot also writes that common Boxer placards in Shantung Province read: "Heaven is now sending down eight million spirit soldiers to extirpate these foreign religions, and when this has been done there will be a timely rain." For the Boxers, White foreigners were "Primary Devils," while Chinese Christians were "Secondary Devils," and all non-Christian Chinese who collaborated with the foreigners were "Tertiary Devils."

The Boxers quickly turned their anger into action on All Saints' Day in 1897. On that day, two German Catholic priests—Richard Henle and Franz Xaver Niles—were hacked to death by members of the Big Swords Society. A third missionary, Georg Maria Stenz, managed to survive despite being himself repeatedly stabbed and slashed with knives and hatchets. Such anti-Christian and xeno-phobic violence was nothing new.

In 1870, an orphanage run by the French Catholic Sisters of

Charity was attacked by hundreds of Chinese men after several Chinese orphans died from an unknown disease. The attackers believed that the European Christians made medicine out of the hearts and eyes of the children. The attackers, who probably engaged in the very same type of traditional Chinese medicine that is currently killing off the world's tiger and rhino populations, also believed that the French nuns were guilty of removing fetuses from Chinese women in order to practice Western alchemy. Given such blood libel, it is not surprising that the mob raped sixteen of the orphanage's nuns, removed their eyes, cut off their breasts, and threw their chopped up bodies into the burning flames of the orphanage itself.[2] Other such attacks would plague northern and central China up until the Boxer Rebellion of 1900.

The Boxer hatred for foreigners proved to be mutual. Preston notes that most of the journal entries and letters written by the European citizens of the various legation quarters of Peking speak of the rampant filth of the city and its citizens. Words and phrases like "the worst smells imaginable," "dusty and malodorous," and "disgusting" appear frequently.[3] This revulsion often translated into haughty treatment of locals by European missionaries or diplomats. Also, European leaders like Kaiser Wilhelm II of Germany promoted the idea of the "yellow peril," or the belief that rising Chinese birthrates and huge waves of Chinese immigration to places like Australia, Canada, and the United States was a direct threat to Western civilization. The Kaiser invoked such ideas when he sent his men to China in 1900, reminding them that they belonged to a superior civilization and superior martial culture.

A great task awaits you: you are to revenge the grievous injustice that has been done. The Chinese have overturned the law of nations; they have mocked the sacredness of the envoy, the duties of hospitality in a way unheard of in world history. It is all the more outrageous that this crime has been committed by a nation that takes pride in its ancient culture. Show the old Prussian virtue. Present yourselves as Christians in the cheerful endurance of suffering. May honor and glory follow your banners and arms. Give the whole world an example of manliness and discipline."[4]

At the apex of his speech, Kaiser Wilhelm promised his men that "prisoners will not be taken." Other leaders from London to St. Petersburg followed suit, while the American and British press penned lurid stories about the various crimes carried out against Westerners in China by roving bands of Boxers. For the Boxers, European Whites practiced a barbaric religion that sacrificed children and used burnt corpses to sanctify the many railroads that they built. This is why, on December 31st, 1899, the British Reverend Sidney Brooks was murdered and had his detached head thrown into the dirt by Boxer thugs. To their White adversaries, the Boxers represented the "savagery" of the East that needed to be conquered by Christian civilization. An armed confrontation was inevitable.

The rebellion began in the winter of 1900, and by May that year, a large Boxer army had Peking surrounded. Trapped inside of the city were hundreds of European, American, and Japanese citizens, including women and children. Chinese Christians, who told the Europeans about how the Boxers wantonly killed all Christians and burnt down their churches, also found refuge in the besieged legation quarters and the few Christian churches manned by foreign troops in Peking.

Despite years of misinformation, Richard Bassett notes in *For God and Kaiser* that Austro-Hungarian sailors received and fired the first shots of the Siege of Peking. Typically portrayed as cowardly or incompetent, the sailors of the Dual Monarchy (almost all of whom were ethnic Croats) brought a Maxim machine gun to the battle and did much to shore up weak French and Belgian lines. With only 420 men in total, the Austro-Hungarians punched above their weight against thousands of Boxer rebels and uniformed Chinese troops. Elsewhere, hundreds of British, French, Belgian, German, Japanese, and Russian legation guards tried to keep the Boxers out of the foreign quarter. However, by June 13th, the Boxers were in full control of Peking and pillaged the city. As they burned Christian churches and destroyed European shops, the Boxers chanted "Sha! Sha!" (Kill!

Kill!).[5]

The "yellow" presses of America and Great Britain warned the English-speaking world in July 1900 that 1,800 White men, women, and children had been murdered in Peking by the Boxers. These stories provided chilling accounts about torture and mutilation. The West had to respond; the newspaper editors demanded. Even though this mass murder did not actually happen following the capture of Peking, the specter of White women and children being butchered by Boxers provided enough motivation to goad a foreign coalition into being.

The first major offensive from the West came in the form of the Seymour Expedition. 2,100 British sailors and 112 US sailors and Marines led by Admiral Edward Seymour of the Royal Navy landed at Tientsin. Although the expedition did manage to kill several Boxers on the first day, the small Anglo-American force never made it out of Lang-fang and thus the foreign citizens trapped inside of the city had to wait until another relief expedition could reach them.

Other military offensives proved more successful, such as the taking of the Taku Forts outside of Peking. While the combined British, Italian, German, Russian, American, Japanese, and Austro-Hungarian forces moved towards Peking, their compatriots in the city managed to hold off against Boxer forces for a total of fifty-five days. Similarly, the coalition marched on Tientsin and captured the city on July 14th.

The battles for Peking and Tientsin eerily presaged World War I and the difficult art of conducting coalition warfare. In some instances, the coalition barely functioned at all. When the march on Tientsin began on June 4th, 1,700 Russians decided to leave their allies behind at camp to take the city all by themselves. Their ill-advised rush into battle halted before 50,000 enemy troops, many of them Chinese regulars. The Russian retreat was covered by 140 US Marines commanded by Littleton Waller. The Marines earned great distinction by battling it out with the Qing forces, and four enlisted men earned the Medal of Honor for their part in the running shootout.

Near the end of the Battle of Peking, European vanity once again trumped common sense when US soldiers commanded by

General Adna Chaffee were ordered to stop their advance into the Forbidden City. The men of the 14th Infantry Regiment had fought tooth and nail against Qing defenders and had lost six dead and nineteen wounded. When the order came down, US soldiers had just passed the final gate of the walled fortress. Officially, the leaders of the expedition did not want US forces to capture Empress Dowager Cixi, despite the fact that she had given official support to the Boxers and had sent hundreds of crack Chinese Muslim fighters (the "Kansu Braves") into Peking. The Europeans simply wanted all participating soldiers to march through the Forbidden City at the same time two days later.

During such black comedy, some true heroes distinguished themselves. All military commanders noted the discipline and bravery of the Japanese soldiers involved in the fighting, and unlike their German and Russian colleagues, Japanese troops did not indulge in rape and looting after Peking was retaken. US Marine Captain John Twiggs Myers stayed up for several days in a row to direct the defense of the Tartar Wall inside of Peking during the siege. Myers only left the wall when he contracted typhoid fever after accidentally stepping on a Boxer spear.

Other notable men included Marine Private Dan Daly, a future winner of two Medals of Honor. During the siege of Peking, Daly spent an entire night on the Tartar Wall by himself. With just a 6mm Lee Navy rifle, Daly managed to fend off hundreds of Boxer and Qing Army troops. When he was relieved the next day, he told his fellow Marines that the Chinese had called him *Quonfay* ("devil") all night long. Another plucky American trooper was Corporal Calvin P. Titus of the 14th Infantry. At Tung Pien Gate outside of Peking, Titus scaled the wall by himself and used his rifle to suppress Boxer and Qing troops. This allowed his fellow soldiers to enter the city and eventually break the siege.

The Boxer Rebellion played an outsized role in geopolitics between 1900 and 1945. As part of the $335 million indemnity placed on the Qing Empire, the Russian government decided to take Port Arthur and occupy all of Manchuria. This in turn angered Tokyo, which sought to expand Japanese economic power throughout East Asia. The Russo-Japanese War of 1904–1905 not only helped to cause the proto-Bolshevik revolution of

1905, but it also showed millions of Asians that White soldiers were not invincible. The victorious Japanese would later feed into this idea by completely dehumanizing captured Allied POWs and White civilians living in conquered territories. Keep in mind: the Japanese march against European power in Asia began when Japan first marched through Manchuria in 1931 and the rest of coastal China in 1937.

The Boxer Rebellion also opened a historical wound on the Chinese psyche. Chinese students today still learn about the foreign soldiers who committed sacrilege by marching through the Forbidden City. The Chinese Communist Party also used the example of the Boxers to encourage the machinations of the Red Guards. During the Cultural Revolution, which may have killed as many as two million Chinese citizens, Chinese Communists sang songs about ridding China of all foreigners. Like the Boxers before them, the vanguard fighters of the Cultural Revolution participated in a planned and orchestrated uprising predicated on superstition and a belief in a false religion (this time Communism instead of folk customs).

China, which is today in the ascendancy, sees the Boxer Rebellion and the entire nineteenth century as a great age of shame. To avenge that shame, China must again reclaim its proper place as the "Celestial Kingdom." Given that Maoism and the Chinese Communist Party spent the 1960s and 1970s giving guidance, weapons, and money to anti-White terrorist groups in Africa, Asia, and Latin America, a resurgent China might not bode well for a Western civilization that is currently on the ropes.

[1] Boot, Max, *The Savage Wars of Peace: Small Wars and the Rise of American Power*, Revised Edition (New York: Basic Books, 2014): 72.
[2] Mungello, D.E., *Drowning Girls in China: Female Infanticide in China since 1650* (New York: Rowman & Littlefield, 2008): 58.
[3] Preston, Diana, *The Boxer Rebellion: The Dramatic Story of China's War on Foreigners That Shook the World in the Summer of 1900* (New York: Walker & Company, 2000): 162.
[4] Kaiser Wilhelm II, "Hun Speech (1900)," *German History in Documents and Images*, http://ghdi.ghi-dc.org/sub_document.cfm?document_id=755.
[5] Thompson, Larry Clinton, *William Scott Ament and the Boxer Rebellion: Heroism, Hubris and the "Ideal Missionary"* (Jefferson and London: McFarland & Company, 2009): 7.

White Hats, White Fighters

American Renaissance, October 13th, 2017.

At The Edge of the World: The Heroic Century of the French Foreign Legion
By Jean-Vincent Blanchard
Bloomsbury Press, 2017
262 Pages

The French Foreign Legion seems like a fighting force made for Hollywood. With its white hats (*kepi blanc*), sharp uniforms, and its reputation for enlisting men with no place left to go, the Legion seems like the stuff of romance.

Jean-Vincent Blanchard, a French Studies professor at Swarthmore College, portrays the Legion during what is widely considered its golden age—roughly from 1880 until 1939. In Professor Blanchard's telling, the Legion was neither a complete band of rogues, nor a fully modern military force. Yes, these men were professional soldiers, and many fled troubled lives in their native lands to seek money, pleasure, and danger in the Legion. Many joined to escape bourgeois culture and create a männerbund (a competitive, hierarchical group of men).

Some of the Legion's leading officers supported this anti-modernist attitude. General Hubert Lyautey comes close to being the central figure of Blanchard's fascinating study. A native of Lorraine with noble ancestry who attended France's Saint-Cyr military academy, Lyautey was a staunch Catholic, a conservative supporter of *Action Française*, and a sworn enemy of the "decadent" Third Republic. He became the Legion's greatest leader during the age of France's colonial expansion. Lyautey once summarized his personal politics as "incompatible with egalitarian and collectivist society."[1]

For Lyautey and other French generals who were drawn to the Legion, it provided an alternative to France's stultifying materialism. For these men, life—real life—was fighting Bedouin or Tuareg tribesmen in the desert of Morocco or putting down Tonkin pirates. One of the Legion's most famous recruits, a German youth named Ernst Jünger, saw it as a chance to break away from the stifling boredom and conformity of a wealthy, peaceful Europe:

> *Those young persons who, in the foggy dark of night, left their parental home to pursue danger in America, on the sea, or in the French Foreign Legion. It is a sign of the domination of bourgeoisie values that danger slips into the distance.*[2]

Such romantic idealism was often the first casualty of life in the Legion. After signing up for their first five-year enlistment and undergoing basic medical examinations, Legionaries received their first lodgings at Fort Saint-Jean in Marseilles. Described by Blanchard as "imposing and gloomy," this fortress offered recruits their first taste of strict military life. From here, recruits were put on ships for the training camps in French Algeria.

For Legionnaires, basic training including marching, rifle practice, physical training (including boxing), and more marching. The only perks of these days were the showers, the French bread, the meat stews, and the liberal portions of Algerian wine. The Legion ran on wine and strong coffee, the latter of which was ordered with shouts of "Au jus! Au jus!"

When not marching, Legionaries peeled potatoes and cleaned their barracks. The Legion prided itself on neatness and order, which is a far cry from their daredevil image.

Besides idealists who got their first taste of the strenuous life, the Legion often attracted Europe's criminals, but Blanchard is quick to note that the idea that the Legion accepted murderers is mostly based on German propaganda from before the outbreak of the First World War. The *Bat' d'Af* were the penal regiments made up of the French Army's nastiest criminals, and because they often shared the North African deserts with the Legion, many people confused the two. The Legion did accept some petty criminals or those who had gotten into trouble with other armies, but rarely did they ever provide a new identity to a wanted murderer, rapist, etc.

The German government promoted the idea of a criminal Legion because approximately two-thirds of the Legion's soldiers were Germans or Austrians. A survey of the First Regiment of the French Foreign Legion found in 1897 that out of 7,066 soldiers, there were 1,612 Frenchmen, 1,551 men from German-controlled Alsace-Lorraine, and 1,441 Germans.[3] France kept the German Legionnaires busy fighting in the colonies rather than in the trenches of Europe during the Great War.

And there was a lot of fighting that needed to be done in the colonies between 1914 and 1918. The Legion became prized for their superior fighting skills, their ability to travel light, their maneuverability, and their reputation for fighting to the bitter end. No battle is more enshrined in Legion legend quite like the siege of Camaron, in Mexico, in 1863. On April 30th, Captain Jean Danjou and sixty-three Legionnaires found themselves surrounded by a larger force of Mexican republicans. The Legionnaires fought until only a few were left standing. Their Mexican opponents called them "demons" because of their fierceness.

Blanchard describes in excellent detail how France's conquest of Morocco lasted from 1912 up until the last Berber holdouts were shelled into submission in 1931. By that time, Lyautey, the face and mind of France's "oil slick" concept of slow, hearts-and-minds colonization, was no longer leading the Legion.

Besides his in-depth portrayal of the many campaigns of the Legion, from the conquest of Tonkin to the horrors of counterinsurgency in Madagascar, Blanchard's book is worth reading for its sociological study of the Legionnaires themselves. They were hard-drinking men who usually spent their paydays visiting cafes and brothels. They were also exceptional builders whom Paris used as combat engineers. Foreign travelers often marveled at Legion-built forts and villages, while Legion deserters who fought with the Berbers in Morocco built stone huts that were far superior to those of the natives.

"To be a soldier in the Tonkin or in the Moroccan *bled* (countryside), no matter who you were, a private or a marshal, was to seek remediation toward a lost unity, even transcendence," Blanchard writes.[4] For Frenchmen, transcendence meant leaving behind the gross secularism and socialist politics of the Third Republic. For all Legionnaires, it meant transcending petty nationalism in favor of recognizing a shared European identity. This supra-national identity was forged fighting non-Whites, and like British soldiers fighting their own colonial wars, many Legionnaires though about race in terms that would horrify today's Western youth. Legionnaires in Tonkin called their enemies "pirates" and "bandits," and wrote in their diaries about how both Vietnamese and Chinese insurgents lived off of the sale of women and opium.

In Indochina, Legionnaires fought a murky insurgent war against an enemy that could easily blend in with the local peasant population. One veteran wrote about how the Legion approached the problem of distinguishing between friend and foe:

> *We were allowed to kill and plunder everything when the villagers did not show up to submit. We left at night around ten or eleven, we went to villages and surprised the people in bed. We killed everything, men, women, children, at gun butt and with the bayonet, it was a real massacre.*[5]

As brutish as the war in Tonkin was, for Legionnaires service in East Asia was often looked upon as a reward. After all, in Tonkin, Annam, and Cochinchina, Legionnaires had access to attractive prostitutes, warm beaches, and the splendid sights of Buddhist pagodas ringed by green mountains. Legionnaires generally considered the Vietnamese and southern Chinese as dirty and ignorant but respected their ancient cultures.

North Africa was a different story. Even during the nationalist antagonisms engendered by World War I, French and German Legionnaires had no problem joining forces to fight the hated Arabs. Although their French officers often celebrated the heroism of the Arab and Berber tribal fighters of Algeria and Morocco, the soldiers under them frequently saw the French "pacification" in racial terms. After all, the Legion was for only for White men at this point, with native recruits put into their own formations like the Zouaves and Skirmishers. Even today, although the Legion's doors have been opened to non-White recruits, a type of racial realism exists in the minds of Legion officers. One unnamed officer told *Vanity Fair* journalist William Langewiesche that: "the Chinese make the worst Legionnaires," while "Americans and British are almost as difficult, because they get upset about living conditions." Ultimately, in today's Legion, the "French are flaky, the Serbs are tough, the Koreans are the best of the Asians, and the Brazilians are the best of all."[6]

Blanchard reveals that Legionnaires, for all their bluster and hard-boiled cynicism, were prone to *le cafard*, a type of nihilistic depression that often led to suicide. In the section on the conquest of Madagascar, Blanchard cites tales about Legionnaires hanging or shooting themselves after battles or long marches. The dreary repetitiveness of sloughing through the hot sun on little food or water caused many Legionnaires to give up hope. Others decided that life as the sharp end of the French spear was not to their liking. Without battle, many Legionnaires became apathetic and unconcerned with their own lives.

Multi-ethnic Legionnaires came to identify the Legion as something more important that their national origins, and all recruits were united by race. Blanchard notes that it did not take much to inspire Legionnaires to fight Arabs because they despised them. Legion veterans also backed reactionary or nationalist causes. Jean-Marie Le Pen, who founded the National Front, was a Legionnaire. Imperialist diehards who participated in the Algiers Putsch of 1961 and the terrorist group OAS were all directly tied to the Legion.

Blanchard's book is an excellent look at one of history's most exciting military units during its heyday. However, it is marred by poor syntax and grammatical errors. It is hard to believe an editor even touched this volume.

The Legion, which is a small, elite force in the French Army, has played an outsized role in modern French history. The United States has nothing like it.

---

[1] Blanchard, Jean-Vincent, *At the Edge of the World: The Heroic Century of the French Foreign Legion* (New York & London: Bloomsbury, 2017): 170.

[2] Blanchard, *At the Edge of the World*, 102.

[3] Ibid., 103.

[4] Ibid., 217.

[5] Ibid., 63.

[6] Langewiesche, William, "The Expendables," *Vanity Fair*, 12 Nov. 2012.

THE PLAN OF SAN DIEGO

American Renaissance, November 1st, 2019.

San Diego, Texas is a tiny, nondescript town in the deep south of Texas. As of the US census of 2010, fewer than 5,000 people live there. Unsurprisingly, most of these residents speak Spanish and have deep roots in Mexico. The Texas borderlands have been this way since the Texas Revolution, and thanks to mass immigration from Mexico and Central America, Texas, and the rest of the South and Southwest, move closer towards the Hispanic cultural orbit every day.

Despite the hopes and dreams of Catholic Integralists like the Iranian convert Sohrab Ahmari or Harvard Law professor Adrian Vermeule, the latter of whom once wrote that a just immigration policy in the United States would "disproportionately favor immigrants from Africa, Asia, and Latin America" so long as they are "confirmed Catholics," a more Hispanicized America means more Santa Muerte cultists, more Santeria practitioners, and more drug-addled gangsters with avowed appreciation for Satan and all his cruel works. Even church-going Hispanics are more likely to believe in Liberation theology, which combines socialism with anti-White vitriol. This is our future so long as our current elite remains in power.

Back in 1915, the United States got a terrible glimpse of its future, and that glimpse occurred in San Diego, Texas. On January 6th, 1915, a manifesto appeared in San Diego (then having a population of 2,500 people, 75 percent of whom were Hispanic).[1] Later dubbed the Plan of San Diego, the Spanish-language document called for nothing less than a race war against all Anglo Texans:

On the 20th day of February, 1915, at two o'clock in the morning, we will arise in arms against the Government and Country of the United States of North America, ONE AS ALL AND AS ONE, proclaiming the liberty of individuals of the black race and its independence of Yankee tyranny which has held us in iniquitous slavery since remote times. . . .[2]

Despite the invocation of "the black race," the purpose of the Plan of San Diego was to turn South Texas into an independent republic controlled by the Hispanic population. Under the banner of "Equality and Independence" and lead by the so-called "Liberating Army For Races and Peoples," the rebels, who were given the Spanish name of *Seditionistas*, hoped that by shedding Yankee blood, the new Hispanic republic in Texas would rejoin Mexico. Thus, the plan argued, the stain of the American victory of 1846–1848 would be removed and "North American imperialism," which had taken Mexican territory "in a most perfidious manner," would be humbled.[3]

The plan called for an independent republic in the Southwest for Blacks, as well. The Apaches were to be respected and given Anglo land, while, in the manifesto's strangest passage, the Japanese were singled out for inclusion in the Hispanic and Black war against Anglo Whites. In general, the Plan of San Diego, which was signed by Mexican nationals and US citizens of Mexican ethnicity, sought an ethnic cleansing of English-speaking Whites in Texas and the Southwest, and wanted Hispanic, Black, Indian, and Japanese (but not Chinese) soldiers to do the killing.

Tensions between Anglos and Tejanos were already long-simmering by the winter of 1915. According to Benjamin Heber Johnson in *Revolution in Texas*, "The United States' conquest of the Mexican north was a traumatic event for the conquered, often bringing dramatic, wrenching changes."[4] These changes were first and foremost demographic. In California, for example, "the Gold Rush drew immigrants from all of the states of the Union and from places as diverse as south China, Chile, Sonora, England, France, and Belgium." [5] The same story played out in Arizona and Colorado. The one exception was New Mexico, which managed to cling to its Spanish Creole heritage, culture, and character well into the twentieth century. (These days, even though New Mexico was once home to proud conquistadors and their offspring, a majority of phenotypically White New Mexicans are self-identifying as Hispanic rather than White.)

In Texas, the Anglo takeover began in the 1830s. At the famous Battle of the Alamo, English-speaking Texans (called "Texians") were joined in their fight for Texas independence by US citizens from the South and frontier states like Kentucky and Tennessee, as well as immigrants from Denmark and Great Britain.[6] Tejanos also fought at the Alamo and for Texas independence, but the revolution turned into a race war once General Antonio Lopez de Santa Ana, Mexico's answer to Napoleon Bonaparte, made it his military mission to "rid Texas of its Anglo-Celtic colonists."[7]

After the Texian victory and the incorporation of the Republic of Texas into the United States, the formerly Mexican province assimilated into the wider culture of the American South. Texas would later supply the Confederate Army with some of its best fighting men, including the fearsome Kentuckian John Bell Hood and his Texas 4th Infantry. However, despite this cultural transformation, South Texas, especially the border region of the Nueces Strip, retained its Mexican character. In this region, which included the tiny village of San Diego, Tejano cattle barons used an Old World-style patronage system that included Anglo machine politicians that relied on Hispanic votes. Often well-to-do Anglo and Tejano families intermarried, and many Anglo settlers converted to Roman Catholicism. This did not present much of an issue, for the Tejano elite of south Texas were proud of their Spanish heritage. Also, as Johnson notes, "a cultural and material egalitarianism strongly marked [Texas] society."[8]

Things began to change once the railroads opened South Texas to more immigrants. Suddenly, within a few years, the Nueces Strip was home to thousands of English-speaking farmers, laborers, and boomtown types. These new arrivals "were generally blind to differences among the ethnic Mexican population," and many saw Spanish-speakers as a source of cheap labor and nothing else.[9] Such economic and cultural displacement led to bad blood, but economics alone cannot explain the antipathy towards

Anglos found in the Plan of San Diego. After all, the seventh point in the manifesto demanded that "Every North American over sixteen years of age shall be put to death."[10] What then was driving the signers of the Plan of San Diego towards ethnic cleansing?

One cannot understand the Plan of San Diego without recognizing that it was part of the wider Mexican Revolution. And like the Plan of San Diego, the spark of the Mexican Revolution was a manifesto penned by Mexicans living in Texas (San Antonio to be exact). In the *Plan de San Luis Potosi*, Mexican revolutionaries, angered by the arrest of liberal politician Francisco Madero, called for a military uprising against General Porfirio Diaz, the conservative strongman who had been in control of Mexico since 1884. The call to revolution was answered by warlords in the north and south. Men like Pascual Orozco and Pancho Villa orchestrated ambushes aimed at terrorizing the Federal army, while Emiliano Zapata took aim at the rural politicians, or *caciques*, in the south. Within a year, Ciudad Juarez was in rebel hands and Madero was declared Mexico's new president.

As is usually the case in the Third World, the revolution turned against itself. Zapata broke from Madero over the latter's refusal to grant land to Indians, while Orozco and Villa likewise turned against the staid liberal for not reforming Mexico fast enough. The revolution of 1910 fractured into multiple civil wars, with army officers and bandit leaders carving up fiefdoms throughout the country. Army general and the warlord of Mexico City, Victoriano Huerta, looked poised to take advantage of the situation when, in February 1913, he was installed as the country's president following a backroom deal that included Madero and US Ambassador Henry Lane Wilson. Once in power, the drunken tyrant Huerta had Madero executed. Madero's death kept the revolution going, as the *Plan de Guadalupe* was issued and called upon Huerta to step down as Mexico's president. An uneasy alliance between Villa, Zapata, Alvaro Obregon, and Venustiano Carranza eventually broke into open warfare in 1915.

Throughout the Mexican anarchy, Mexican fighters and refugees traversed the American border with ease. South Texas became a den of spies, with pro-Villa and pro-Carranza forces carrying out assassinations with impunity. One of the men involved in both revolutionary intrigue and the Plan of San Diego was Basilio Ramos. It was the arrest of Ramos, an ardent Huerta supporter, in McAllen, Texas that lead to the discovery of the Plan of San Diego, for Ramos was one of the document's nine signers.[11] Besides Huerta's intelligence network in Texas, other possible participants in the Plan of San Diego included the anarchist Ricardo Flores Magon and men known to be followers of Carranza. Indeed, historians Charles H. Harris III and Louis R. Sadler have uncovered conclusive proof that the Plan of San Diego was an "instrument of Mexican government policy" authorized by Carranza's government, distributed by Mexican secret agents like Juan K. Forseck, and partially financed by the Royal Brewing Company of Kansas City, which was at that time owned by Jack Danciger.[12] Danciger, a Jewish American, was not only one of Carranza's biggest supporters in the United States, but also the owner of *El Cosmopolita*, a Spanish-language newspaper that acted as Carranza's mouthpiece in the US.[13]

Other foreign nationals were deeply involved in the Plan of San Diego as well. Lincoln Steffens, the Progressive "muckraker" and future apologist for the Soviet Union, worked at *El Cosmopolita*. Although not as well-known as Steffens, the German mercenary Felix Sommerfeld, who had earlier deserted from the US Army, used his influence in the Carranza military to try and get Captain Karl Boy-Ed, the German naval attaché in Washington, to listen to his half-cocked plan to instigate a war between the United States and Mexico.[14] A large part of this plan, which would play a significant role in the infamous Zimmermann Telegram, would include German support for Mexican irredentism in Texas and the Southwest. Specifically, Mexico and Mexican nationalists in the US were promised all the land that they had lost in 1848 if they waged war against the United States. This war included the race war found in the Plan of San Diego.

Ultimately, despite widespread reports of German agents across the US-Mexican border, the Bureau of Investigation (the precursor to the FBI) failed to find any serious evidence of Berlin's involvement in Mexico City. Rather, the BOI, which maintained the Old Mex 232 file on microfilm, did find evidence of extreme race hatred against Anglo Texans. The Plan of San Diego was the match that finally lit the powder keg.

Beginning in the summer of 1915, Mexican rebels and bandits began crossing into the lower Rio Grande valley, where they carried out thefts, kidnappings, and murder.[15] *Sedicionistas* from Mexico and Texas "launched some 30 raids against ranches, railroads, telegraph lines and other targets in the border region, killing nearly two dozen US citizens."[16] One horrific incident saw these raiders kidnap, torture, and decapitate a US soldier before displaying his detached head on a pole overlooking the border.[17] Then, on January 10th, 1916, Villa and his men captured a train near Chihuahua City. Onboard were American miners returning to Mexico to work in American-owned mines. Villa and his men told all the Mexican passengers to leave the train. Seventeen of the eighteen Americans were then murdered in cold blood.[18]

These horror stories forced President Woodrow Wilson to mobilize half of the entire US Army to the US-Mexican border in November 1915.[19] Furthermore, the Department of Justice urged President Wilson "to arrest [Luis] De la Rosa and [Aniceto] Pizana and to restrain local Constitutionalist [pro-Carranza] commanders who seemed to be sanctioning the raids."[20] De la Rosa and Pizana were Tejanos who were active in trying to get Tejanos and Mexicans to join forces in an anti-Anglo uprising in the Nueces Strip. They were also involved in the creation of the Plan of San Diego. Further urgency towards action was felt in Washington following another Mexican border raid, this one occurring in Columbus, New Mexico.

Just after 4 a.m. on March 9th, 1916, Pancho Villa and approximately 500 mounted rebels stormed into Columbus with shouts of "Muerte a los gringos!" For two to three hours Villa's men set fire to buildings, attacked civilians, and attacked members of the 13th US Cavalry stationed at Camp Furlong. Although caught off guard by the raid, the men of the 13th Cavalry bloodied Villa's men during several hand-to-hand engagements. One unknown private rushed at the Mexicans, and despite being shot in the stomach, managed to kill three Mexicans before dying. When Villa's men entered the camp's kitchen, Army cooks attacked them with shotguns, boiling water, and axes. Across town, a barefoot lieutenant roused his men and their French-made Benet-Mercie machine guns and got them to rain fire down on every sombrero they could see.[21] When it was finally over, the death toll included ten American civilians, eight American soldiers, and about 80 Villistas.

The Columbus raid angered the American public so much that they demanded that President Wilson punish Villa for his actions. 140,000 National Guard soldiers were sent to secure the border, and under the leadership of General John "Blackjack" Pershing, the Punitive Expedition was carried out across the border and deep into northern Mexico. Pershing's expedition, along with an offensive carried out by Carranza's army, managed to kill 400 Villistas in just three months.[22] While the Army failed to capture Villa, they did clear northern Mexico of his followers.

Back across Rio Grande, things were still volatile. On New Years' Eve, 1918, in Nogales, Arizona, Private John Andrews of the 35th Infantry shot and killed Mexican national Francisco Mercado as he tried to illegally cross into the United States. This killing would be just one episode in a larger racial war that would last until August 1918. Following a series of tit-for-tat shootings, Mexican soldiers and armed civilians attacked the border on August 27th. The fact that the Mexicans were supported by machine gun nests and snipers located in the Sonoran hills points to the fact that the assault had been planned.[23] Later dubbed the Battle of Ambos Nogales, five US soldiers and one American civilian were killed, while thirty Mexican soldiers perished. The battle ended at 7:45 p.m., when American soldiers and civilian auxiliaries saw a white flag fluttering in the Sonoran hills. This part of the border would remain contentious until both sides agreed to construct a two-mile wall separating Nogales, Arizona from Nogales, Mexico.

Much of this bloodshed was the direct result of the Plan of San Diego and the perfidy of the Mexican government. It was Carranza's government, specifically Emiliano Nafarrate, the army officer in charge of keeping the peace on the Mexican side of the Rio Grande between Brownsville and Laredo, Texas, who "permitted Plan [of San Diego] activities within his area and actively sponsored them."[24] This unholy mixture of revolutionary activity, racial grievance, and corrupt politics inspired a brutal response from Anglo Texans and the Texas Rangers. "Extralegal executions became so common," Johnson notes, "that a San Antonio reporter observed that the 'finding of dead bodies of Mexicans . . . has reached a point where it creates little to no interest.'"[25] This Anglo violence forced many Tejanos to drop their Mexican identity in favor of a Mexican American one.

This uneasy truce would hold until the 1960s. Mexican radicals began eschewing all things American in favor of an unvarnished Mexican nationalism and "brown pride." The theory of Aztlan, which is central to movements like La Raza and others, seeks to resurrect the mythical Aztec homeland by "returning" the American Southwest to Mexico. The Plan of San Diego is one of the foundational documents of Aztlan thinking, as Mexican radicals living in the US see in mass immigration and demographic displacement a version of the warfare demanded by the 1915 manifesto. One of the first casualties of this racial *reconquista* could be Texas.

How can American patriots stop this bleak future? The most obvious answer is to demand that our government follow in the footsteps of President Wilson and send a huge military contingent to the border. Rather than police the deserts of the Middle East or the jungles of Africa, where the populations seem incapable of saying "Thank You," our military would be better served by securing our border, which in turn would help to secure the future of the historic American nation. Deportations and repatriations are a must, and our government needs to get serious about investigating Mexican meddling in American politics. Despite what we hear day in and day out about Russia and Ukraine, in reality Mexico, Qatar, Israel, and China are the biggest corruptors of the American body politick.

On a more profound level, not only does the United States need a serious rejection of political correctness and anti-White idiocy, but so too does Mexico. Since declaring their independence from Spain, Mexico has been at constant war with itself and its identity. Since the end of the Mexican Revolution in 1920, Mexican populists and left-wingers have done everything in their power to deny their nation's European heritage. Rather than celebrate

Hernando Cortes, who, with just 600 soldiers and sixteen horses, "destroyed the empire of Montezuma," [26] modern Mexico and Mexicans would rather idolize the bloodthirsty Aztecs and their kingdom built on human sacrifice. The insanity runs so deep that the Mexican government, which has long been in the hands of the White *castizo* minority, is planning to host an international summit on the dire threat of "White supremacy" in the United States. Such an action can only be seen as part and parcel of the wider desire among left-wing Latin Americans to strike at the Yankee colossus by supporting *mestizo* supremacy as a replacement for European heritage.

Mexico and the United States were both established by European Christians as lands for themselves and their progeny. Liberalism, false egalitarianism, and racial grievance mongering have obscured this fact. To stop the Plan of San Diego from becoming anything more than a piece of history, nationalists and patriots in both countries need to resurrect and defend our European inheritance—one born from the swords of Castilian conquistadors and the other from the blood and toil of frontiersmen drawn from the British Isles, the Netherlands, and cold forests of Northern Europe.

---

[1] Charles H. Harris III and Louis R. Sadler, *The Plan de San Diego: Tejano Rebellion, Mexican Intrigue* (Lincoln: University of Nebraska, 2013): 1.
[2] Harris and Sadler, *The Plan de San Diego*, 2.
[3] Ibid.
[4] Benjamin Heber Johnson, *Revolution in Texas: How a Forgotten Rebellion and Its Bloody Suppression Turned Mexicans into Americans* (New Haven and London: Yale University Press, 2003): 10.
[5] Ibid.
[6] Stephen L. Hardin, *Texian Iliad: A Military History of the Texas Revolution, 1835–1836* (Austin: University of Texas Press, 1996): 152.
[7] Ibid.
[8] Johnson, *Revolution in Texas*, 15.
[9] Ibid., 39
[10] Harris and Sadler, *The Plan de San Diego*, 3.
[11] Rolando Hinojosa Smith, "River of Blood," *Texas Monthly*, 1 Jan. 1986.
[12] Harris and Sadler, *The Plan de San Diego*, x, 13.
[13] Ibid., 14.
[14] Thomas Boghardt, "Chasing Ghosts in Mexico: The Columbus Raid of 1916 and the Politicization of U.S. Intelligence during World War I," *Army History*, No. 89 (Fall 2013): 11–12.

[15] James A. Sandos, "Pancho Villa and American Security: Woodrow Wilson's Mexican Diplomacy Reconsidered," *Journal of Latin American Studies*, Vol. 13, No. 2 (Nov. 1981): 295.

[16] P.G. Smith, "Divided Against Itself," *Military History*, Vol. 36, No. 4 (Nov. 2019): 35–36.

[17] Ibid.

[18] Ibid.

[19] Sandos, "Pancho Villa and American Security," 295.

[20] Ibid., 296

[21] Boghardt, "Chasing Ghosts," 7.

[22] Sandos, "Pancho Villa and American Security," 303.

[23] Smith, "Divided Against Itself," 37.

[24] Sandos, "Pancho Villa and American Security," 297.

[25] Johnson, *Revolution in Texas*, 3.

[26] J.H. Elliott, *Imperial Spain, 1469–1716* (London: Penguin, 2002): 63.

A Little-Known Chapter
In the Muslim War Against the West

American Renaissance, August 23rd, 2019

The two great colonial powers of Europe, Great Britain and France, faced massive Islamic uprisings in the Middle East in the aftermath of World War I. Beginning around 1920, Arab fighters, who took plenty of inspiration from the poorly thought out words of President Woodrow Wilson's "Fourteen Points,"[1] briefly put aside their tribal and sectarian divisions in order to bring battle against both London and Paris. In British Mesopotamia (today's Iraq), approximately 131,000 Shia and Sunni tribesmen in the Middle and Lower Euphrates regions carried out raids, ambushes, and several sieges on isolated British outposts mostly manned by Indian soldiers. In one particularly bloody incident in July 1920, hundreds of men of the 108th (Indian) Infantry Regiment and the Manchester Regiment were massacred at night near the Rustumiyya Canal.[2] The British Empire's hold on Iraq would remain perilous until the capture of the holy city of Najaf in August 1920. Even after this victory, which was accomplished thanks to five Indian divisions and two British infantry divisions (1st Battalion, Rifle Brigade and 2nd Battalion, East Yorkshire Regiment), the newly formed Royal Air Force had to keep several squadrons in the country and resorted to dropping poison gas on the more recalcitrant tribes.

The British predicament in Mesopotamia was partially inflamed thanks to outside actors. Namely, as the British were fighting in Iraq, British, French, Armenian, and Greek soldiers were also fighting Mustafa Kemal's nationalist forces in Turkey. The Kemalists made no secret that they considered the Iraqi city of Mosul Turkish territory. The British wanted Mosul in Iraq. The

Turkish nationalists, however, could not directly aid their Muslim brethren fighting the British. Rather, Bolshevik agents in Turkey and Persia provided weapons and money to both Kemal and the Arab insurgents. The Russian Communists even established the *Jam'iyyat Takhlis al-Sharq al-Islami* (Organization for the Liberation of the Muslim East) for the purpose of "supporting and encouraging the struggle of Muslim peoples against European domination."3

The Bolsheviks also published the now infamous Sykes-Picot Agreement in 1917 to stir up anti-imperial sentiment in Asia and Africa. Wittingly or not, Western professors and journalists continue to ape the Bolshevik line that the modern Middle East's boundaries are the work of know-nothing Europeans, even though Sykes-Picot was a dead issue by 1919. Furthermore, in his excellent book *The Ottoman Endgame*, Professor Sean McMeekin articulates that "the partition of the Ottoman Empire was not settled bilaterally by two British and French diplomats in 1916, but rather at a multinational peace conference in Lausanne, Switzerland in 1923."4 Neither Sykes (who died of the Spanish flu in 1918) nor Picot played any role at Lausanne, and indeed the real mover and shaker, and thus the true architect of the modern Middle East was none other than Mustafa Kemal himself. The contemporary obsession with Sykes-Picot, McMeekin points out, has more to do with postcolonial theory and a desire to bash European imperialism than with actual history.

At the same time as the British were busy fighting Iraqi Arabs, the French were fighting Syrian Arabs. Called the Franco-Syrian War of 1920, the French sent in thousands of soldiers, most of whom were a mix of Arab, Senegalese, and French Foreign Legion troopers, to overthrow the short-lived Arab Kingdom of Syria. Several years after the French took Damascus, a new enemy arose in the secretive Druze mountaineers. John Harvey, a Welsh coal miner and former British soldier who joined the French Foreign Legion in the 1920s, recounts the ferocious fighting between the French Foreign Legion and the Druze in his great book, *With the French Foreign Legion in Syria*. In Harvey's testament, he has a lot of terrible things to say about the French and the Foreign Legion, but most of his venom is reserved for the Senegalese.

Harvey describes these Black soldiers, whom Paris used to fight its small wars in the colonies, as less than useless. During action at Rashaya, the "black troops were in a state of hopeless panic" and had to be whipped into fighting by their White officers.[5] The only time when the Senegalese showed any thirst for fighting was when a squad of them could torture a wounded Arab or Druze. Harvey makes it clear that it took France two years to put down the Druze revolt because of the poor quality of her West African troops.

A third imperial power spent the 1920s putting down an Islamic rebellion. That power was none other than Spain, once the greatest empire in human history. By 1920, Madrid's colonial possessions were a pale shadow of more glorious days. Former possessions in South and Central America had been gone since the 1820s, while the American victory in 1898 saw the loss of Cuba, Guam, Puerto Rico, and the Philippines. For Spanish colonialists looking to enhance Madrid's prestige, the only option left was to conqueror and expand in northern Morocco.

Spain has a long and mostly violent relationship with Morocco. In the early eighth century, Visigothic Spain was overrun by an Islamic army officered by Arabs but mostly made up of Berber tribesmen native to Morocco. According to Cuban American historian Dario Fernandez-Morera, the Muslim invasion of Spain began with a Berber raid in 710. A Berber haul of beautiful Visigothic and Hispano-Roman female slaves inspired the Umayyad governor Musa ibn Nusayr to lead his army into the Christian kingdom.[6] The Umayyad conquest of Spain not only saw an inferior civilization triumph over a superior one (Morera uses Arab, Greek, and Latin texts, plus recent archaeology, to highlight that the Visigoths were literate and skilled administrators who built fabulous roads and churches all the while maintaining Spain's Roman heritage), but it was only accomplished thanks to treachery carried out by a Byzantine count in North Africa named Urbanus or Julian and the Jews of Spain. The Muslim army of conquest left the latter group in charge of captured cities like Cordoba and Toledo.[7]

The Catholic Visigoths managed to hold out against the Muslim invaders in the northern Kingdom of Asturias. Following the

Visigothic victory at the Battle of Covadonga, Christian armies undertook the *Reconquista* to reclaim Spain for Christendom. The Visigothic nobles of Asturias and Leon led the first wave of reconquest, while Castile and its ally in Aragon finalized the reunification of all of Spain in 1492. Despite the current idiocy about Muslim tolerance and multiculturalism in Spain, Islamic Spain believed in and practiced jihad, which its Maliki jurists defined only as warfare or violence in the name of Islam. The most vicious Muslim tyrants of Spain were the Berber Almoravids and Almohads. The Almoravids expelled the entire Christian population of Andalusia to Africa in 1106 and 1138, while the Almohads exterminated the remaining Christian population of Granada and gave both Christians and Jews the options of either conversion or death.[8] The Almoravids and Almohads were both Moroccan dynasties.

Even before Spain was totally free from Muslim rule, Spanish and Portuguese Christians brought the fight to Morocco. In 1415, King John I of Portugal conquered the Marinid city of Ceuta. Ceuta would remain in Portuguese hands until the city was formally ceded to Spain by King Afonso VI in 1668. Melilla fell to Spanish arms in 1497, five years after King Ferdinand and Isabella took over the Nasrid Kingdom of Granada, the last Muslim state in Spain. These two autonomous port cities would be the sole representatives of Spanish authority in North Africa until 1860. In that year, Spain won a short war in Morocco whereby Morocco's sultan officially recognized Ceuta and Melilla as Spanish cities. Between 1893 and 1894, Spain once again defeated a Moroccan army, this time demanding that the sultan do a better job of policing the notoriously rough and rebellious Rif Berbers who lived near Melilla.

Spanish expansion in Morocco did not fully begin until 1910, when Spain's Army of Africa extended Melilla's territory to a piece of Mediterranean coastland called Cape Three Forks. In 1912, Morocco was divided between a French-occupied zone that included the major cities of Fez, Rabat, and Casablanca and the Spanish Protectorate of Morocco, which was a thin stretch of coastline connecting Ceuta and Melilla. Two great obstacles stood in the way of complete Spanish control over northern Morocco: 1) the endemic corruption and cynicism of the Spanish government and many Spanish Army generals, and 2) the Berber inhabitants of the Rif Mountains.

The land of the Rif Berbers is a "land of barren mountains and deserts, rarely unified or pacified, chronically misruled, [and] inhabited by a fanatically xenophobic population made up largely of primitive Muslim tribesmen."[9] The Rif Mountains in 1920 were an area so rich in tribal blood feuds that most family homes contained fortified blockhouses for defense. The Berbers of the Rif were proud of their independence, and worse for the Spanish and French was the fact that the Rifian Berbers were durable soldiers and excellent marksmen who were skilled in guerrilla warfare. These traits would make the natives of the Rif arguably the best insurgents that any colonial power faced in the twentieth century.

The first Europeans to make serious headway with the Rif tribes were the Germans. German steamers in Melilla provided "1,500 to 2,000 tons" of goods to Moroccans in 1913 alone,[10] while German merchants mastered Arabic and built post offices, railroads, telegraph lines, and other modern conveniences for the Rifian Berbers. In exchange, German conglomerates sought access to the mineral deposits that many Europeans believed existed underneath the Rif Mountains. The Germans also saw potential allies in the Rif Berbers, and during World War I, German arms and money flooded into the Rif as part of a plan to encourage Moroccan tribesmen to invade French Algeria. France, in response, deployed much of its Foreign Legion to Morocco during the Great War, while Great Britain provided support to the Spanish as part of their larger plan to keep the French well away from Gibraltar.

Between 1912 and 1920, it was mostly quiet in the Spanish Protectorate. The average Spanish soldier serving in Morocco believed that "the Moors were sworn enemies of all Christians" and that Madrid was a civilizing force in a barbarous land.[11] Arturo Barea, one of these Spanish soldiers, would later denounce Spain's occupation, saying with mockery, "'Civilize the Moroccans . . . we? We from Castile, Andalusia, Gerona, who cannot read or write? Nonsense! Who is going to civilize us?"[12] Barea, who characterized Spanish colonialism in Morocco as part battlefield and part brothel, echoed the frustration of the average Spanish soldier serving in the Rif. Conditions for these troops were deplorable. Even after army-wide raises in 1918 and 1920, most Spanish officers had to take second jobs. Non-commissioned officers and conscripts enjoyed barely edible food, few if any medical services, and notoriously poor hygiene standards, all the while being paid about a penny a day. Most of the infantrymen who landed in Morocco were completely untrained, too.

These poor conditions were made worse by corrupt and inept officers. Promotion was usually given to the most senior army officers, not the most experienced or bravest. The Spanish Army was also overloaded with officers, a majority of whom preferred garrison life in Spain to the hazardous mountains of the Rif. In September 1922, during the height of the war in the Rif, officers in the Larache Sector of the Spanish Protectorate were caught embezzling over a million Spanish pesetas ($143,000) in funds and supplies.[13] Privates and sergeants often resorted to selling their Mauser rifles and ammunition in local markets in exchange for fresh fruit and vegetables. Many of these guns would later kill thousands of Spanish soldiers.

The only effective fighting force defending the Spanish Protectorate was the new Spanish Foreign Legion. Nicknamed the Tercio, the Spanish Foreign Legion was created in January 1920 and was intended to be Madrid's version of the French Foreign Legion. Like its French counterpart in Algeria, the Tercio's home was in North Africa. The Tercio drew adventurers of all kinds, including Spaniards, exiled Russian noblemen, a few criminals, and at least one Black American.[14] The soldiers of the Tercio were paid sixty cents a day and could look forward to enlistment bonuses between seventy-five and one hundred dollars. With their extra money and superior *esprit de corps* (the Tercio went into battle shouting "Long Live Death"), the Tercio were Madrid's shock troops during the Rif War, fighting 845 battles between 1920 and 1927. One of their number, a middle-class Galician by the name of Francisco Franco, not only distinguished himself as a brave and fearless Tercio officer, but would ride his success to becoming a general at the age of thirty-three.

The Tercio could not save Spain from the major blunders that defined the early war in the Rif, however. By 1920, the Berber tribes of the mountains were ready to revolt against both the French-backed sultan and the Spanish soldiers guarding Ceuta and Melilla. The leader who unified the Berber tribesman was named Abd El Krim. Born in the village of Ajdir near Alhucemas Bay on the Mediterranean Sea, Abd El Krim attended Spanish schools in Melilla as a boy and studied the Koran in the holy Moroccan city of Fez. In 1906, Abd El Krim took his first job as the editor of the Arabic supplement to the Spanish-language newspaper, *El Telegrama del Rif*. The future insurgent and self-declared Amir ("prince") of the Republic of the Rif began his path towards Rifian nationalism while teaching Arabic to Spanish students in Melilla. Here, Abd El Krim realized that the mineral potential in the Rif ought to be exploited by the local Berbers, not the Spanish. Furthermore, Abd El Krim sought a national state for the Rifian Berbers, who, unlike their neighbors, had never been Arabized. This ideal state would practice sharia law, but would also include European advisors for the purpose of instructing the backwards Rifians in European medicine and science. By the summer of 1921, Abd El Krim's tribal army of the Rif included between 3,000 and 6,000 men. These numbers would soon deal a massive blow to the 45,000-plus Spanish soldiers in Morocco.

In July 1921, Abd El Krim's Berber army attacked most if not all the Spanish forts running from Buy Meyan to Dar Drius. The two men in charge of the Spanish forces in the Rif, General Manuel Fernandez Silvestre and General Damaso Berenguer, were very different from one another. Silvestre was a fight-first imperialist who, in 1921, was busy using his army to increase the size of the Spanish Protectorate. Berenguer was a more circumscribed officer who had tried in vain to get the civilian government in Madrid to do something about the sorry state of the Spanish Army. Silvestre and Berenguer did share two things in common: they were both born into military families in Spanish Cuba and both underestimated the Rifian threat.

On July 17th, 1921, thousands of Berber guerillas poured down on the Spanish forts and garrisons. Many of these fortifications were miles away from the nearest water supply, and thus some of the Spanish soldiers had to rely on drinking pimiento juice, vinegar, cologne, ink, and the collected juices of tomato cans.[15] Relief columns sent down from the Spanish fort at Anual were ambushed and massacred. Anual itself was raided and seized. Silvestre was killed in the fighting (some sources say he committed suicide), while thousands of Spanish soldiers were shot in the back as they fled or were hacked to death by sword-wielding Berbers. The Rifian offensive was so successful that by August 1921, thousands of Berber tribesmen and *mujahidin* were camped in the outskirts of Melilla. Only the fact that Rifian Berbers were unused to urban life, let alone urban warfare, saved the residents of the Spanish city.

The bloodletting of the summer of 1921 was atrocious. After the exhausted, starving, and dehydrated defenders of Monte Arruit surrendered after weeks of fighting, the Berbers rushed into the fort and stabbed every Spaniard to death. The Rifians cut so many Spanish throats that they became bored with the slaughter. All told, the disaster of 1921, which has become known as the Battle of Anual, cost 13,192 Spanish lives and saw the loss of 20,000 Mauser rifles, 400 machine guns, and 129 cannons.[16] The disaster at Anual was so shocking to the Spanish psyche that King Alfonso XIII backed a military coup led by the Andalusian General Miguel Primo de Rivera in 1923. De Rivera (who advocated for Spain to abandon Morocco) blamed the liberal civilian government for not providing enough money to the Spanish Army. De Rivera was also tapped by the military and the monarchy as the one man strong enough and popular enough to control Spain's greatest internal weak point—Catalonia. Under De Rivera's dictatorship, Catalan separatists, many of whom refused to go to Morocco after being called up from the reserves, were arrested and banned from conducting street protests. De Rivera's government also hit upon a military solution to the Moroccan quagmire. Namely, Spanish garrisons that could not be easily defended would be abandoned. The Tercio would continue to take the fight to the Berbers, while less experienced and raw recruits from Spain would undergo intensive training in the fortified cities of Ceuta and Melilla.

De Rivera's plan met with sharp criticism from the *africanista* faction, which wanted Spain to stay and fight in Morocco to uphold Spanish prestige. The *africanistas* got plenty of ammunition during De Rivera's planned retreat which began in 1924. After abandoning the few blockhouses that had not fallen to Abd El Krim's forces, retreating Spanish soldiers visited heaps upon heaps of festering corpses that had not been buried since Anual. Spanish soldiers came upon bodies that had been violated by stakes wrapped in barbed wire, bodies that had had their eyes and genitals removed, beheaded bodies, bodies that had been sawed in half, and even bodies where entrails had been used as makeshift handcuffs.[17] While De Rivera's plan was ultimately successful, it came at a heavy cost. During the fighting of 1924, the Rif Berbers not only captured the city of Chaouen and forty miles of Spanish territory, but thousands of Spanish soldiers died during fighting retreats that featured Berber snipers firing from the high ground. In one instance, 500 *legionarios* under the command of Franco were killed during the last day of the retreat.

The year 1924 would prove to be the high point of the Rif rebellion and its leader. The international city of Tangier, where British and American businessmen dominated, briefly threw support behind Abd El Krim and allowed munitions and food to pass through to the Rif Mountains. World opinion saw Abd El Krim as an underdog fighting for the freedom of his people. The Islamic world was even more effusive in its praise for the Rifian rebels, with many would-be Islamic insurgents taking inspiration from the Rifian fight against European Christendom. Another group that wholeheartedly supported the Rifian rebels were Europe's Communists. According to John Cooley, Jacques Doriot (later founder of the fascist French Popular Party) and the French Communist Party sent aid to the rebels, while the Comintern in Moscow sent two agents, Sharif Mulay Hasanov and Namber Mahmudov, to Abd El Krim.[18] El Krim, a man whose money mostly came from German entrepreneurs and who used violence and terror to keep tribes loyal to his movement, played up his anti-imperial credentials by sending a letter to a convention of Latin American leftists comparing his war against Spain with their own wars of independence.

Even amid his successes, Abd El Krim was in a precarious position. After all, south of the weak Spanish Protectorate was the leviathan known as French Morocco. Here, better-trained, and better-equipped French soldiers, including the Foreign Legion as well as the usual Senegalese and Arab units, enjoyed warm relations with the Berber tribes. The man in charge of French Morocco was General Louis Hubert Lyautey, France's greatest colonial soldier. Lyautey, who had seen action in French Indochina, Algeria, and Madagascar, believed in letting the Berbers and Arabs run their own affairs. He also believed that the French had a duty to improve the lives of the locals, and under his administration, the French military in Morocco built hundreds of schools, railroads, hospitals, and banks. The problem for the French was that the Rifians did not recognize the borders between the French and Spanish zones, and thus the two sides began fighting one another in 1924.

Despite all their advantages and despite their belief in their innate superiority to the Spanish Army, the French fared no better against the Rifian Berbers early on. Indeed, by July 1925, the Rifians had captured forty-three out of sixty-six French posts in eastern Morocco. They also nabbed 51 cannons, 200 machine guns, 5,000 rifles, and 35 mortars.[19] Franco-Spanish fortunes only turned following the amphibious landing at Alhucemas Bay on September 8th, 1925. Here, 13,000 soldiers, the vast majority of whom were Spanish, led by General Jose Sanjurjo and General Philippe Petain took the all-important beachhead near the Rifian capital of Ajdir. Led by the Tercio, it took the Spanish troops weeks to remove well-placed Rifian snipers and artillery from the many caves all above the bay. In the skies, the French *Escadrille Cherifienne*, which was made up of American volunteers like Lieutenant Colonel Charles Kerwood and Lt. Col. Austin Parker, provided the Franco-Spanish invasion force with air cover and plenty of bombs. After this bloody victory and the destruction of Ajdir, the Republic of the Rif was as a good as dead. Rather than surrender to the Spanish, who would have surely executed him, Abd El Krim surrendered to the French in 1926. He would be exiled to the French island of Reunion for over twenty years. While there he received a generous stipend courtesy of French taxpayers.

The Rif War, which formally ended in mid-1927, is remembered today as one of the first instances of Moroccan nationalism. The modern kingdom and its people see in Abd El

Krim one of their founding fathers, even though the Rifian Berber despised Morocco's traditional Arab ruling class. After achieving independence from France and Spain in 1956, the Moroccan government approached Abd El Krim in exile in Cairo and asked him to return home. The old insurgent refused because there were still French, Spanish, and American soldiers stationed in Morocco. As for the Rifian Berbers who came close to pushing the Spanish out of Morocco for good, they rebelled against the independent Moroccan government starting in October 1958. Upset that so few government positions were occupied by Rifian natives, members of the Beni Urriaguel tribe created the Popular Movement and the Rif Movement for Liberation and Liquidation in order to break away from the secular and religious monopolists in Rabat and Fez. Ironically, one of the biggest complaints of the Rifians in 1958 was the fact that the new government replaced the familiar Spanish language with the alien French. [20] For their desire for independence, Rifian Berbers had wet cement shoved up their rectums by troops and policemen far more brutal than either the French or Spanish.

As for the Spanish, they may occasionally enjoy a good period drama set during the Rif War, but for the most part they are more concerned about the colonization of their homelands by Moroccan "migrants." In 2018, the ruling Socialist Party in Madrid welcomed more than 64,000 migrants. This human wave earned the Socialists a crushing defeat in Andalusia, where the upstart right-wing party Vox began to generate momentum thanks to its anti-immigration stance. On April 28th, 2019, Vox won twenty-four seats in the Spanish general election—a fine showing for a party's first time. Vox and other patriotic movements in Spain will only continue to rise thanks to increased immigration, anarcho-tyranny (several days ago in Barcelona, six North African men had the rape charges against them dropped because the fourteen-year-old Spanish girl they assaulted was drunk and did not "fight back"), and the constant anarchy in Ceuta and Melilla, where sub-Saharan Africans continue to pour in and tax the already broken Spanish immigration system. Something must be done.

If Spaniards want to keep their identity and their glorious history, which includes not only the conquest of the New World but also the victory in the Rif, they must find the courage of their ancestors and defeat the new Moors trying to destroy the Spanish crown, the Spanish faith, and the Spanish blood.

[1] Ian Rutledge, *Enemy on the Euphrates: The Battle for Iraq, 1914–1921* (London: Saqi, 2015): 134–135

[2] Rutledge, *Enemy on the Euphrates*, 293–311.

[3] Ibid., 177

[4] Sean McMeekin, *The Ottoman Endgame: War, Revolution, and the Making of the Modern Middle East, 1908–1923* (New York: Penguin Books, 2015): xx.

[5] John Harvey, *With the French Foreign Legion in Syria: Fighting with the Legion of the Damned* (London: Greenhill Books, 1995): 176–177.

[6] Dario Fernandez-Morera, *The Myth of the Andalusian Paradise: Muslims, Christians, and Jews under Islamic Rule in Medieval Spain* (Wilmington, Delaware: ISI Books, 2016): 20.

[7] Fernandez-Morera, *The Myth of the Andalusian Paradise*, 38.

[8] Ibid., 186

[9] David S. Woolman, *Rebels in the Rif: Abd El Krim and the Rif Rebellion* (Stanford: Stanford University Press, 1968): 3.

[10] Woolman, *Rebels in the Rif*, 9.

[11] Ibid., 57

[12] Ibid.

[13] Ibid., 108

[14] Ibid., 68

[15] Ibid., 90

[16] Ibid., 96

[17] Ibid., 103

[18] John Cooley, *Baal, Christ, and Mohammed: Religion and Revolution in North Africa* (New York: Holt, Rinehart and Winston, 1965): 191–193.

[19] Woolman, *Rebels in the Rif*, 182.

[20] Ibid., 226

"God wills, man dreams, the work is born."

The opening lines of Fernando Pessoa's poem "Prince Henry the Navigator" invoke what Pessoa himself termed "mystical nationalism." Like Pessoa the man and creator, this term has various and multi-faceted meanings.

On the one hand, a biographical note left behind by Pessoa defined a "mystical nationalist" as a man against Communism and socialism. This man also holds views that are deeply "anti-reactionary." How can this be, especially given Pessoa's poetic odes to the heroes of Portugal's imperial past?

Like British poet Hugh MacDiarmid and the transatlantic T.S. Eliot, Pessoa sought to use the Modernist revolution in letters, which supposedly freed artists from past restraints of meter and form, to capture a profound sense of Portuguese identity. As Eliot's "The Wasteland" summarizes the abject poverty of a new Western world without God or traditions, Pessoa's *Message* collection articulates a desire for a rebirth of lost glory.

In order to fully appreciate the later work of the mad poet Pessoa, one must not only understand him—that archetypal flaneur of Lisbon whose face and image adorn a million coffeehouses—but also the former imperial greatness of Portugal.

Pessoa was not your average Lusitanian. After the death of his father, his family relocated to British South Africa, where Pessoa excelled in English language schools. A born writer, Pessoa began contributing to South African newspapers at a tender age. Upon returning to his beloved Portugal in 1905, Pessoa started his rather unusual career as a bon vivant, business translator, and man of letters.

In between bouts of coffee drinking at Lisbon's *Cafe A*

Brasileira, Pessoa wrote a veritable army of unpublished work and helped to run Modernist literary journals like *Orpheus's Generation*. He also keenly observed the dramatic changes that were then altering Portugal forever.

In October of 1910, republicans lead by the writer Teofilo Braga dethroned Manuel II, the last King of Portugal. Like the later Second Spanish Republic, the First Portuguese Republic sought to erase the "stain" of monarchism, reaction, pre-capitalism, and empire with a new system of individual rights, civil rights, and an identity based in an adherence to governmental law.

Like others, Pessoa got caught up in the widespread enthusiasm for the new First Portuguese Republic. As a man of the middle class, Pessoa believed that the republic held the keys to a better economic future. However, such materialist deductions were nothing compared to Pessoa's mystical passions. The poet, according to Darlene J. Sadlier in "Nationalism, Modernity, and the Formation of Fernando Pessoa's Aesthetic," saw in the republic a chance to make a new, modern, and thoroughly Portuguese spirituality. The operational name of this identity was "Republican Sebastianism."[1]

However, Pessoa's support for the republic began to wane. Republican Sebastianism sought to replace the much older belief in Sebastianism, or an imperial faith that the martyred child King Sebastian (who died fighting the Muslims at the Battle of Alcacer Quibir) would return one day to save the nation. Republican Sebastianism, which simply sought to make Portugal a cultural and political power once again, lacked the Christian mysticism of the original. Namely, Sebastianism, which remains a part of reactionary thought in both Portugal and Brazil, sees in the lost King Sebastian, who not only died fighting the hated Moors, but who also kept the tiny Portuguese nation from falling into the hands of the Castilian monarchs, a testament to the God-given glory of the Portuguese nation.

The First Portuguese Republic proved to be a failure all around. Historian Hugh Kay described it as a political order of "continual anarchy." Worse still, the instability of the republic did not deter it from its anti-clerical mission. Led by Prime Minster Afonso Costa, the First Portuguese Republic moved to block the Roman

Catholic Church from pursuing its purpose as a redoubt of arch-conservatism in the face of republican radicalism. As later aped by Spanish republicans in the 1930s, Portuguese republicans enacted the "wall of separation" law in 1911 that closed seminaries, nationalized church properties, ended the observance of several holy days, and secularized burial grounds. In one decisive thrust, the Portuguese First Republic claimed power over both life and death—a power more properly belonging to God and Jesus Christ.

Many point out that rampant fiscal insolvency caused by Portugal's ill-planned involvement in World War I led to the military coup d'état of May 28th, 1926. However, as was seen later in Spain between 1936 and 1939, the deeply conservative Portuguese military, which included some junior officers influenced by Integralism, saw that republicans had created an anti-Catholic, anti-family, and liberal capitalist state that ran contrary to the basic character of the Portuguese people. By purging liberals, republicans, and secularists, the military dictatorship paved the way for the *Estado Novo* ("New State") of Antonio de Oliveira Salazar. The corporatist Catholicism of Salazar's state, which is still derided by scoffing neckbeards in Lisbon and Rio de Janeiro who call themselves Communists, socialists, and liberals, wisely kept Portugal out of the Second World War, oversaw a flourishing and stable economy, and, along with South Africa and Rhodesia, led the good fight against Communism in Africa until 1974. After Salazar's successor was removed thanks to the Carnation Revolution, the great and ancient Portuguese Empire went with him.

By the time he set down to craft *Message*, Pessoa saw in Salazar's state the possibility of achieving a Portuguese Fifth Empire. Importantly, Pessoa envisioned this empire not as a material entity, but as a spiritual one. Pessoa's poem "Prayer" contrasts the bleakness of the Portuguese First Republic ("All we have left, in this hostile silence, / Is nostalgia and the universal sea") with the possibilities of the New State ("Make us reconquer the Distance—of the sea / Or of another frontier we can possess!"). The sea, which Pessoa calls simply the "Portuguese Sea" in another poem, embodies the old Portuguese Empire of Ferdinand Magellan and the poet Luis Vaz de Camoes, the author of the neoclassical epic *The Lusiads*. The new Fifth Empire is made up of both the sea and the new frontier of spiritual and mental life. By directly invoking Camoes in *Message*, Pessoa articulates a desire for a new Portuguese expansion.

Imperium within and imperium without are defining characteristics of the Portuguese nation. The Integralism of order, the church, history, tradition, and hierarchies are the lifeblood of all great peoples, even for known occultists like Pessoa. Even more essential for Portuguese Catholics and for Catholics across the world, the Christian faith is a universal creed. This does not necessarily mean that Christianity is a multiculturalist faith. Rather, Christianity is an imperium whereby ultimate authority over disparate lands and peoples must be submitted to God and the church. This is the ultimate lesson of Pessoa's "mystic nationalism"—Portugal, as the first great Catholic empire to navigate the world's oceans, has a divine right to conquer beyond its Iberian homeland.

---

[1] Sadlier, Darlene J., "Nationalism, Modernity, and the Formation of Fernando Pessoa's Aesthetic," *Luso-Brazilian Review*, Vol. 34, No. 2 (Winter, 1997), 109–122.

THE RACIAL CONSCIOUSNESS OF ROBERT E. HOWARD

American Renaissance, July 6th, 2018.

"The Marchers of Valhalla," a novelette that did not see publication until 1972, is a frighteningly clear parable about the Indo-European soul and its disintegration in the modern world. The story's main character is a Texan named James Allison. Allison is the scion of an illustrious Texas family, and he says proudly to a lovely stranger: "My great-grandfather died at the Alamo, shoulder to shoulder with David Crockett. My grandfather rode with Jack Hayes and Bigfoot Wallace, and fell with three-quarters of Hood's brigade. My oldest brother fell at Vimy Ridge, fighting with the Canadians, and the other died at the Argonne."[1] Mixed in with pride is shame for Allison. After all, Allison is a cripple who lost his leg at the age of fourteen following a horse-riding accident.

Allison's lameness proves to be an illusion however, for, in a past life, he was Hialmar, a blond and blue-eyed Scandinavian who helped to conquer the Southwest long before the coming of the Spanish. Such a story could only be written by the one and only Robert Ervin Howard.

Howard, who editor Steven Tompkins has dubbed the "Last Celt," was born on January 22nd (some sources say January 24th), 1906. As a child, the Howard family lived in the rough-and-tumble environment of oil boomtowns in Texas. Howard's father was a doctor, while his mother was an invalid who lived in chronic ill-health. Dr. Isaac Mordecai Howard was often gone for long stretches at a time, thus leaving young Robert alone as the soul caretaker for his mother. This close bond between mother and son would play a huge role in Howard's life as well as his untimely death in 1936.

In his letters to fellow pulp writers, Howard often spewed forth venom about life in *noveau riche* Texas. During the 1920s, the Howards lived in Cross Plains, Texas, a north-central town in Callaghan County. Howard knew the city when it was only home to about 2,000 people. However, given the many oil booms that the place experienced, oilmen, riggers, roughnecks, drillers, and other blue-collar workers flooded the area, which in turn led to the growth of bordellos and wanton street violence. Rusty Burke, in a short biography of Howard, said that seeing such rapid change and bloodletting in Cross Plains gave Howard a tough outlook on life. "The influence of this boom-and-bust cycle on Howard's later ideas about the growth and decline of civilization—that societies are built by hardy pioneers, who are then followed by others who grow decadent and enjoy the fruits of the society by contribute nothing to its continued growth . . . has often been overlooked," says Burke.[2]

For the burgeoning writer Howard, the rough, uncivilized men who make up the pioneer races were the ones he idolized most. In his fiction, such men would be the protagonists, and Howard's most famous creation, Conan the Barbarian, is a proudly savage and independent Cimmerian who enjoys violence far more than domesticity.

Similar to the German philosopher Friedrich Nietzsche, who suffered from physical and mental ailments for his whole life, Howard's lionization of masculine strength may have come from his own insecurities. Called a "sissy boy" by others for his bookishness and the novel fact that Howard worked inside all day as a professional writer, Howard was an outcast from Cross Plains society. Howard also took digitalis for his weak heart—a fact which undoubtedly weighed on Howard's mind when, around 1928, he began a serious weightlifting routine and made a study out of boxing. In his short life, Howard was a scholarly recluse and a man of action. He was also a workaday writer who, in the Depression year of 1934, made $1,853.05 (roughly $33,899 in today's money)[3] from just his writing.

Because he was a working writer who was always consciousness of the demands of the pulp market, Howard has often been castigated as a hack by "serious" literary critics. Today,

Howard does not enjoy the reputation of H.P. Lovecraft, the Anglo-Saxon supremacist who rejected the very idea of being a working writer and often discarded stories after one rejection slip. Lovecraft and Howard maintained a strong correspondence during the 1930s. In these letters, both men said things regarding democracy and the races that would see them pilloried and denied publication in today's world. In one fascinating exchange from February 1935, Howard good-naturedly mocked Lovecraft's support for Italian Fascist Benito Mussolini and the very concept of "civilization."

Your friend Mussolini is a striking modern-day example. In that speech of his I heard translated he spoke feelingly of the expansion of civilization. From time to time he has announced; 'The sword and civilization go hand in hand!' 'Wherever the Italian flag waves it will be as a symbol of civilization!' 'Africa must be brought into civilization!' It is not, of course, because of any selfish motive that he has invaded a helpless country, bombing, burning and gassing both combatants and non-combatants by the thousands. Oh, no, according to his own assertions it is all in the interests of art, culture and progress, just as the German war-lords were determined to confer the advantages of Teutonic Kultur on a benighted world, by fire and lead and steel. Civilized nations never, never have selfish motives for butchering, raping and looting; only horrid barbarians have those.[4]

While Lovecraft fretted over the deterioration of Anglo-Saxon civilization in twentieth century America, Howard hated the very idea of civilization itself. For the Texan, civilization was a thin crust—a false reality that overlaid the innate barbarity of man. In one of the author's most famous quotes, Howard claimed that barbarism "is the natural state of mankind. Civilization is unnatural. It is a whim of circumstance. And barbarism must always ultimately triumph." In many ways, Howard was an early anarcho-primitivist, and Tompkins has said that Howard was the penultimate American—a proud offspring of settlers who desired absolute freedom in the wilderness.

Despite his comments in letters to Lovecraft, Howard's fiction often shows an inclination towards some civilizations and peoples over others. Indeed, many of Howard's best stories are about the conflict between masculine, Indo-European civilization and absolute barbarity. "Black Canaan," which was published in the June 1936 edition of *Weird Tales*, the very same magazine that published so many of Lovecraft's stories, sees Kirby Buckner, the son of a powerful local family in the rural South, return home in order to forestall a Black rebellion against their White neighbors. At the heart of the rebellion is the conjure man Saul Stark, a native of South Carolina who claims descent from a witch doctor of the Congo. "Black Canaan" mentions several times the bloody legacy of slave rebellions ("The blacks had risen in 1845, and the red terror of that revolt was not forgotten. . . ."), and Stark's occult power and his desire to turn this slice of the backwoods into a Black stronghold reveals what Howard saw as the innate anti-White hatred and superstitious nature of Blacks. One darkly prophetic scene sees a beautiful quadroon witch tell Kirby of Stark's plan:

> *Those black dogs? They are his slaves. If they disobey he kills them, or puts them in the swamp. For long we have looked for a place to begin our rule. We have chosen Canaan. You whites must go. And since we know that white people can never be driven away from their land, we must kill you all.*[5]

Fortunately, Canaan and the rest of the surrounding lands are populated by the sons of hardy pioneers. These are proud White men, and although they may speak roughly and be a little uncouth, they are ready and willing to defend their lands with their lives.

Another Southern story of horror, "Pigeons from Hell," sees two New Englanders, John Banner and Griswell, come across a zombie residing in a dilapidated Southern mansion. Also set in that swampy region which straddles Arkansas, Texas, and Louisiana, "Pigeons from Hell" concludes that no White American, regardless of their birth, is totally free from the hatred of Blacks.

Another Howard classic, "The Horror from the Mound," which was published by *Weird Tales* in 1932, sees a Texas man named Steve Brill destroying an undead aristocrat who had first come to the Southwest in the sixteenth century. "The Horror from the Mound" puts race realism in blunt words, with Howard writing such things as "Latin-Indian devils had no terrors for the Anglo-Saxon." This story also serves as a reminder for modern American readers that our nation is much, much older than 1776 and the Constitution. Howard's Texas bore European footprints as far back as 1545. Similarly, "The Marchers of Valhalla" makes the case that North America has long been a frontier for Indo-Europeans. The old rivalries between Anglo-Saxon and Celt, Germanic and Latin matter less on the American frontier. Howard's hardboiled heroes reassert their unique and thoroughly American Whiteness while living in the uncivilized borderlands. America is an Anglo-Celtic nation, yes, but its founding stock also includes Spanish and French Catholics and Dutch Calvinists. Americans should not descend into the old, inter-ethnic rivalries of Europe; we are a unique people who should take pride in our Celto-Germanic and Latin (not *mestizo*) civilization. This pride should be our bulwark against the vileness of the modern, multiculturalist world.

Tragically, despite creating brave heroes every day of his life, Howard could not himself transcend sadness. On June 8th, 1936, Hester Howard, Robert's long-suffering mother, slipped into her final coma. When the nurse told Robert that his mother would never regain consciousness, the thirty-year-old writer returned to his Underwood typewriter and penned a short couplet.

All fled, all done
So lift me on the pyre.
The feat is over
And the lamps expire.

Howard then walked to his 1935 Chevy and pulled out a gun. He shot himself but did not die for another eight hours. So ended the life of one of America's greatest writers and visionaries.

Every American man should read the work of Robert E. Howard. Not only do his tales of brave Indo-European men stir the soul, but Howard was also quite capable of penning disquieting and highly literary short stories (see for instance 1931's "The Black Stone"). Howard's heroes, whether they are the Cimmerian Conan, the Texan conqueror of Central Asia El Borak, or the gun fighting Puritan Solomon Kane, remind us that brave White men have always wandered the globe. The Indo-Europeans began as steppe dwellers. Alexander of Macedon and his soldiers captured much of Asia and left behind their blond and light-skinned descendants. Roman soldiers made it all the way to far western China—the very same land that was the ancestral home of the lost red-haired people known as the Sogdians. Indo-Europeans settled North America, Central America, South America, Australia, New Zealand, and southern Africa. Portuguese merchants and priests created the Japanese city of Nagasaki, while Hong Kong and Singapore were created by British men imbued with the love of empire.

This lust for adventure and creation may be dormant in the veins of the modern American male today, but it is still there. Howard certainly knew that, and we, as American nationalists, need to remember it too. After all, this civilization, this kali yuga, is but a temporal thing. It can be overcome by embracing the ancient, the pre-modern, and the masculine. This is what Howard teaches us.

---

[1] Howard, Robert E., "Marchers of Valhalla," *The Black Stranger and Other American Tales* (Lincoln: University of Nebraska Press, 2005): 79.
[2] Burke, Rusty, "A Short Biography of Robert E. Howard," *The Robert E. Howard Foundation*, http://www.rehfoundation.org/a-short-biography/.
[3] Lord, Glenn, *The Last Celt* (Berkeley: Windhover Books, 1976): 75–79.
[4] Qtd. In Doctorow, Cory, "Robert Howard explains the butchersome logic of empire to HP Lovecraft," *boingboing*, 24 Jun. 2014.
[5] Howard, "Black Canaan," *The Black Stranger*, 245.

During the European scramble for African colonies during the late nineteenth century, Italy earned an ignoble distinction. Italy, the youngest and weakest of the "Great Powers," was the only European power to lose a war against an African state. During the First Italo-Abyssinian War, the Ethiopians, who were supported by Russia and France, humbled the poorly led Italians and their mixed Italian and African soldiers, who, out of an approximated 18,000 men, lost 15,000 in casualties. The centerpiece of Italy's humiliation was the Ethiopian victory at Adowa, where, despite losing 7,000 troops, the Ethiopians killed 289 Italian officers, 2,918 Italian soldiers and 2,000 African *askari* (soldiers in Italian employ). Those Italians and *askari* who managed to survive were tortured to death. The lucky few were marched back to Addis Ababa and held as prisoners until Rome paid Ethiopia ten million lire.[1]

After the war, Italy looked to regain not only confidence but also standing in global politics. While the Futurists, a loose collection of artists, poets, and journalists, clamored for machines, speed, and new weapons of war like the airplane, the Italian military was again looking to Africa as the starting point for a renewed empire in Rome. Before long, the Italians were battling the tired and sick Ottoman Turks in Libya.

On September 29th, 1911, the Kingdom of Italy declared war on the Ottoman Empire. Rome's goal was the capture of Tripoli, the Ottoman *vilayet* that included most of today's Libya. While the war is generally regarded as another blemish on Italian military history, "the Italian Army did what the politicians asked of it, and no army could have done much more given the state of technology at the time."[2] Indeed, while General Luigi Capello criticized the war as an "enormous waste of materials,"[3] other Italian officers and European generals marveled at Rome's ability to coordinate ground, sea, and air assaults against the Ottomans and their Libyan militiamen. By war's end Italy owned a significant portion of North Africa and a few islands in the important Aegean.

Despite this pre-World War I success, Italy, which began the war as an ally of Germany, Austria-Hungary, and the Ottoman Empire, ultimately came away from the Versailles conference in 1919 upset over its gains, or rather its lack of them. After all, Italy had joined the Allies after signing 1915's Treaty of London, which guaranteed Italy the Trentino, South Tyrol, the Austrian Littoral (which today includes the Adriatic port of Trieste), parts of Dalmatia, as well as German holdings in Africa. Making matters worse, the Italians had spent the war fighting the Austrians in their own northern provinces without much in the way of help until 1918 when British, French, American, and Czechoslovakian units were dispatched after Germany had sent five divisions in 1917. By that point, after the massive defeat at Caporetto, the Italian Army was hanging on to their front by a thread.

Italy after the Treaty of Versailles reacted a lot like Germany—a defeated power and the legally responsible party for the war. Angered over the Anglo-French sleight, Italian nationalists, many of whom had been pressing Rome towards war with Austria-Hungary in order to claim (or, in their minds, regain) territory throughout the Adriatic and the Alps since the late nineteenth century, seized the moment to redraw the map without the approval of the Allied powers or even the Italian king.

In Fiume, the Italian poet, novelist, and adventurer Gabriele D'Annunzio and several army regiments occupied the city and renamed it the Italian Regency of Carnaro. D'Annunzio and his men capped off their great move by marching to *Ronchi dei Legionari* and pulling off what became known as the *Impresa di Fiume* ("Fiume Exploit.") D'Annunzio had everyone watching Fiume between 1919 and 1920. The move not only heralded a new political force in Italy, but it also put the rest of the world on notice. In Fiume, D'Annunzio created a new free state wherein free love, recreational drugs, and other forms of anarchy commingled with Futurist art and music. Fiume was also a violent place where the

Italian minority maintained a strong rule over the majority Slavs, most of whom were either Slovenes or Croats.[4]

D'Annunzio's experiment did not sit too well with the Italian Kingdom. The Italian government at first refused D'Annunzio's offer to incorporate Fiume into the kingdom. Then, in 1920, Italy and Yugoslavia signed a treaty making Fiume a free state. D'Annunzio refused to recognize this, and during the Christmas week of 1920, his government and its legionnaires were bloodily removed by the regular Italian Army.[5] D'Annunzio loyalists and Communists continued to try and seize Fiume, but finally, in 1924, it was annexed by Italy.

By then Italy had a new leader. Benito Mussolini, a former socialist agitator who remade himself into a Fascist leader and the scourge of the left during the *Biennio Rosso* (1919–1920), borrowed much from D'Annunzio, from his March on Rome in 1922 to trademark oratory style and his over-the-top persona. Although the men eventually grew to despise one another, Mussolini applied D'Annuzio's gamble in Fiume to Rome and, for a while, it worked.

Even though Mussolini shared power with the Italian king throughout his dictatorial reign, everyone knew who was in the driver's seat. When Mussolini talked about a Roman Empire for the twentieth century, political commentators and scribes took him at his word. Italy, Mussolini believed, was destined to be a world power, and with the guiding hand of Fascist corporatism, Italy would remove the shame of Versailles. As such, Ethiopia, one of the very few independent African kingdoms during the age of European imperialism, was targeted for Italian expansion.

The only problem of course was that both Italy and Ethiopia were members of the League of Nations. As such, they had both agreed to Article X of the Covenant of the League of Nations, which guaranteed assistance to any member who was the victim of external aggression. But what about when one member attacks another? Well, in the fall of 1935, that question was answered. Italy won a war against Ethiopia, thus exposing the weakness of the League of Nations.

Like most wars (then and now), the Second Italo-Abyssinian War began as a border dispute. After the Italian forces from Italian

Somaliland built a fort on disputed land, the Ethiopian Empire complained to the League of Nations that the fort violated Ethiopia's sovereignty. This put both powers on high alert, and when the Ethiopian-instigated Wal Wal incident left dead on both sides, war was just a matter of time.

When Emperor Haile Selassie called up the entire Ethiopian army, a large segment of soldiers proved to be underfed and poorly equipped. Even those who carried modern rifles held weapons that were out-of-date and a far cry from the capabilities available to the Italians. Overall, most of the Ethiopian army was poorly trained and outmatched. However, Emperor Haile Selassie did enjoy the use of the thoroughly modernized Imperial Guard, which was armed with Swiss and Czechoslovak weapons, plus it had foreign advisors like the former Ottoman officer, General Mehmet Wehib Pasha.[6]

For the Italians, they could rely not only on those colonial troops stationed in Eritrea and Somaliland but could also bring in regular army and Blackshirt militia units from Italy itself. By the beginning of the war, somewhere in the range of 500,000 Italian servicemen were in the field. With them came some two hundred journalists, making this war a well-covered one.

Besides superior numbers, the Italians also came to Ethiopia with superior equipment, from machine guns to tanks and airplanes, along with naval vessels and motor cars that allowed supplies to travel quickly to units scattered throughout the theater. Finally, besides Italian troops, the Italians also leveraged local tribes as well as recruits drawn from around Africa. Eritrean units saw a majority of the fighting, and as a result suffered most of the casualties on the Italian side.

The Italians were first challenged by Ethiopia's lack of infrastructure and some elaborate fortifications, and they advanced rather slowly from both the north and south. Along the way, the Italians looted Ethiopian landmarks such as the Obelisk of Axum. The largest battle of the war, which took place at Enderta, saw two Italian pincers attack the Ethiopian flanks. In response, the Ethiopians "launched three fierce counter-attacks during the morning and early afternoon," but these attacks were broken by Italian artillery, which included 280 guns that fired 23,000 rounds throughout the battle.[7]

Despite their inferior weapons and manpower, the Ethiopians managed to harass the Italians and even launched the limitedly successful Christmas Offensive of December 1935–January 1936. Here, Emperor Haile Selassie decided to test Marshal Pietro Badoglio, the man who recently replaced General Emilio De Bono, and his two corps of about 125,000 men. The offensive saw about 190,000 Ethiopian troops, almost all of whom were territorial militiamen commanded by local *Ras* (chief), retake several villages and the Tekeze River.[8] This victory not only forced the somewhat overstretched Italians to commit themselves to new counter-attacks, but it also served as a propaganda victory for the Ethiopians. The left-wing press in Europe covered the offensive extensively, while the Black press in America made heroes out of the Ethiopians, who they saw as fighting against worldwide White supremacy. Several hundred Black Americans attempted to volunteer for the Ethiopian armed forces, while Florida-native John C. Robinson became celebrated as the "Brown Condor" who led the Brown Condor Squadron of fliers against the Italians.

Ironically, after breaking the back of the Ethiopians at the Battle of Maychew in March 1936, and after occupying strategic cities, the Italian army successfully abolished slavery in Ethiopia, which initially backfired because the slaves then turned to the Italians for food, shelter, and orders.[9] It was the Italians, who the international left and Black Americans excoriated for promoting racialism and colonial oppression, who actually ended Ethiopia's abhorrent slave trade and the wanton abuse of the Oromo people by the Amharic elite, including the much-lauded Emperor Haile Selassie (who himself owned thousands of African slaves).

The Second Italo-Abyssinian War was the high point of Mussolini's rule. The Italian victory was cheered in Rome, while scholars and politicians throughout Europe quietly (and sometimes not so quietly) began musing whether Fascism really was the future. After the war, Mussolini claimed that: "At last Italy has her empire." And he then added: "The Italian people have created an empire with their blood. They will fertilize it with their work. They will defend it against anyone with their weapons. Will you be worthy of it?" Though the occupation of Ethiopia would prove difficult, bloody, and short-lived, in 1936, the Italians were on cloud nine. That same year, they began sending thousands of troops to Spain to support the Nationalist *putsch*. The *Corpo Truppe Volontaire* (CTV), which numbered approximately 75,000 Italian troops at its peak, provided essential support to General Francisco Franco's armies. Italian soldiers bore the brunt of the Nationalist victories at Malaga in 1937, plus they provided far more assistance than the German Condor Legion at Santander in 1937, during the Aragon Offensive of 1938, and the decisive Catalonia Offensive of 1938–1939. And just a few months before the start of World War II, Italy again repeated itself, this time capturing and occupying Albania.

These successes only served to hide Italy's glaring weaknesses though. Never as economically capable as Germany, the Italians grew to rely on their northern ally for manufacturing and military assistance after disastrous blunders in North Africa and Greece. By 1940, Italy was reduced to the same position as Austria-Hungary in World War I. It became Germany's burden to bear— its tiresome ally who could not contribute much to the overall war effort. In fact, because of Italian losses in North and East Africa as well as the Balkans, Hitler's forces had to come to the rescue, thus tying down a large portion of the German army throughout the war's duration.

Even though Italy became one of the war's lesser lights, in 1936 it was considered the primary aggressor in Europe and Africa. Most commentators would have figured Italy as the spark for World War II in Europe, not Germany. Also, as the big tiger of the mid-1930s, the Italians commanded respect and fear, and their war in Ethiopia completely undermined the League of Nations, exposing it as a sham defense force.

---

[1] Greg Blake, "First Italo-Abyssinian War: Battle of Adowa," *HistoryNet*, https://www.historynet.com/first-italo-abyssinian-war-battle-of-adowa.htm.
[2] Charles Stephenson, *A Box of Sand: The Italo-Ottoman War 1911–1912* (Ticehurst, East Sussex, UK: Tattered Flag, 2014): vii.
[3] Stephenson, *A Box of Sand*, 227.
[4] Leopold Froehlich, "A Poetic Regime," *Lapham's Quarterly*, July 19, 2017.
[5] Janez Jansa, "Bloody Christmas," *reakt.org*, https://web.archive.org/web/

20120402022400/http://www.reakt.org/fiume/pdf/011_bloody_christmas.pdf.

[6] "Clash of Monarchies: The Second Italo-Abyssinian War," *The Mad Monarchist*, Jan. 29, 2017, http://madmonarchist.blogspot.com/2017/01/clash-of-monarchies-second-italo_29.html.

[7] John Gooch, *Mussolini's War: Fascist Italy From Triumph to Collapse, 1935–1943* (New York: Penguin, 2020): 25.

[8] George Baer, *Test Case: Italy, Ethiopia, and the League of Nations* (Stanford: Hoover Institute Press, 1976): 176.

[9] "The Italian Empire, A History to Take Pride In," *The Mad Monarchist*, July 27, 2016, http://madmonarchist.blogspot.com/2016/07/the-italian-empire-history-to-take.html.

FIGHTING THE YELLOW PERIL

American Renaissance, August 2nd, 2019.

In the 1932 film *The Mask of Fu Manchu*, the vile Dr. Fu Manchu (played by Boris Karloff) addresses an assembly of Asian warlords. Thanks to his theft of the golden death mask of Genghis Khan (which, it should be added, was found by British archaeologists), the warlords have proclaimed Fu Manchu as their new leader. The cruel Manchu's triumphant speech exposes the intentions of his new pan-Asian empire: "Conquer and breed. Conquer the white man . . . and take his women!"

Even in 1932, when Britain, France, the Netherlands, and the United States had colonial holdings all throughout Asia, such blatant racialism was controversial. MGM, the studio that produced the film, fired director Charles Vidor after seeing an early draft. MGM worried that the censors would have a field day with the film's gratuitous scenes of torture and drug use. MGM was also worried that the film would antagonize America's Chinese community, especially given such bold pieces of dialog as Dr. Van Berg (played by Jean Hersholt) skeptically asking, "A Chinamen beat me?" or Sir Dennis Nyland Smith (played by Lewis Stone) saying, "Do you suppose for a moment Fu Manchu doesn't know that we have a beautiful white girl here with us?" (For his part, Karloff's Fu Manchu calls the Englishmen "son(s) of a white dog!")[1]

Many of the currently available versions of *The Mask of Fu Manchu* have been edited to weaken the overtly racial message of the film. Unedited versions can be found online, but buyers must be knowledgeable. The film's racialist message, which articulated the idea that the Orient and the Occident will forever be at war with each other and the East seeks to defeat the West biologically, came right from the pen of Sax Rohmer, the working-class and Irish Catholic Brummie who created the character of Dr. Fu Manchu in his 1913 novel, *The Mystery of Dr. Fu Manchu*. Rohmer's creation is widely credited with popularizing the literary genre of the "Yellow Peril," or a type of pulp fiction that makes use of Orient vs. Occident themes in vulgar ways.

Since the rise of cultural Marxism and the New Left of the 1960s, Asian scholars have earned praise and, more importantly, grant money and status by railing against the Anglo pulp fiction of yesteryear. Whole books and classes are dedicated to the "paranoia" of anti-Asian sentiment and the "pervasive" racism of Western society towards Asians. In a serene bit of irony, the first state to successfully silence Rohmer's "Yellow Peril" yarns was Nazi Germany in 1936. Although Rohmer clarified that "my stories are not inimical to Nazi ideals," the Third Reich still banned *Dr. Fu Manchu* as both degenerate and the work of a suspected Jew.

Given that the postwar period saw the creation and proliferation of Asian activism in the European colonies and the West itself, it is surprising that Yellow Peril stories kept being told. Besides Count Dracula and Frankenstein's monster, Sir Christopher Lee made Hammer Film Studies wealthy by portraying a slew of villainous Chinese characters, from Chung King in 1961's *The Terror of the Tongs* to Fu Manchu himself in 1965's *The Face of Fu Manchu*, 1966's *The Brides of Fu Manchu*, 1967's *The Vengeance of Fu Manchu*, 1968's *The Blood of Fu Manchu*, and 1969's *The Castle of Fu Manchu*. In every instance, Lee's diabolical Manchu is defeated by lily-White British men.

Even earlier, a new comic series debuted with an unabashedly imperialist and Yellow Peril story. Created by the Belgian illustrator Edgar P. Jacobs, the Blake and Mortimer series began on September 26th, 1946 with the publication of a short story called "The U Ray" in *Tintin* magazine. "The U Ray" would be redesigned and expanded to become *The Secret of the Swordfish* in 1950. The final graphic novel in the popular series would be published in 1953. [2] The story arc introduced Jacobs's two principle characters—the Scottish scientist Philip Mortimer and his friend Captain Francis Blake of MI5. Blake and Mortimer, much like the Hammer films of the 1950s and 1960s, added a gloss of futurist technology and some modern sensibilities to otherwise deeply Victorian tales. Call this pop culture archaeofuturism, but the popular Blake and Mortimer series tapped into a populist European desire to maintain the order, stability, and glory of their colonial empires (the British Empire in the case of this series).

As with all subsequent Blake and Mortimer stories, the main antagonist in *The Secret of the Swordfish* is the criminal adventurer Olrik. Olrik, with his thin and curled mustache and slick black hair, was based on Jacobs himself. In *The Secret of the Swordfish*, Olrik is a mercenary colonel of Hungarian ancestry in the service of the Yellow Empire of Basam Damdu, an egomaniacal dictator headquartered in the fabled Tibetan city of Lhasa. Like Fu Manchu, Emperor Damdu is hell-bent on reducing the White world to ashes. Damdu and his Yellow Empire is based on the Japanese Empire of the Second World War, and the East Asian Buddhist and Arab Muslim soldiers of Damdu's army all dress in Imperial Japanese army uniforms.

While a lot of voices on the Dissident Right praise Japan as an ethno-centrist state and even go so far as to defend Japan's efforts in World War II, Jacobs and his generation had no such illusions. They knew that the officer corps of the Japanese army saw it as their divine mission to "lead the people of Asia out of slavery to the white man."[3] This meant not only invading British Hong Kong, British Singapore, British Burma, French Indochina, the Dutch East Indies, and American Philippines, but it also meant forcing White POWs to clean Chinese and Korean streets like common laborers.[4] This was done to humble the Whites in front of Asian crowds. The interment and rape of White and Eurasian families on Java was done for similar reasons.[5]

From Potala Palace, Emperor Dambu launches state-of-the-art rockets, jet fighters, and paratroopers. The forces of the pan-Asian Yellow Empire seek to outdo Genghis Khan. As a result of his empire's initial success, Emperor Damdu brags that "Rome, the eternal city, is only a memory. . . . Paris, the city of light has been utterly crushed. . . . The proud metropolis of London has been turned to ash." The Yellow Empire forces the British Empire, its colonies, and its American allies to their knees, but the West is far from defeated.

Thanks to the pluck and courage of European, American, and colonial Indian soldiers, as well as the deployment of Mortimer's one-of-a-kind Swordfish jet fighter, the Yellow Empire is overthrown, Basam Damdu dies after a *Gotterdammerung* of his own making in Lhasa, and the ever resourceful Olrik flees to fight another day. In the stories immediately following *The Secret of the Swordfish*, Olrik winds up in British Egypt as a conman before becoming a babbling wild man in the deserts of the Anglo-Egyptian Sudan.

Jacobs died at age eighty-two in 1987. Since then, Belgian writers and cartoonists have kept the Blake and Mortimer characters alive in comic books and on television. The imperialism of the Jacobs originals is still alive and well too. Written by Yves Sente and drawn by Peter Van Dongen and Teun Berserik, *The Valley of the Immortals*, which was translated into English just last year, returns to the Yellow Peril themes of *The Secret of the Swordfish*. Here, General Xi-Lee, a ruthless Chinese warlord based in the country's south, believes that he is the direct descendant Qin Shi Huang, the legendary first emperor of China. As such, Xi-Lee wants to use this lineage and the recently discovered treasures of the first emperor to unite all of China under his rule. This would include taking over Hong Kong and Portuguese Macau. Blake and Mortimer, along with anti-communist Chinese (Xi-Lee has allied himself with Mao), fight the good fight from the European outpost in Hong Kong, which is still British in the story.

Other post-Jacobs graphic novels are equally reactionary. 2010's *The Voronov Plot* denounces Soviet Communism and all those who seek the resurrection of Stalinism. 2013's *The Septimus Wave* features as one of its antagonists Dr. Kim Ku-Dum, a Korean and a former torturer in the service of the Yellow Empire. Overall, in the new stories and the reprints and translations of Jacobs's originals, the British Empire still rules the world and Asia is still not to be trusted.

A direct line can be traced from Fu Manchu to Basam Damdu to Xi-Lee. All three villains see the world as a battleground between the West and East, and all three are committed to overthrowing everything White and replacing it with everything

Yellow. These men are cruel and vicious, but Blake and Mortimer always find a way to win in the end. These stories remain popular and even critically celebrated today. In 2004, Paris's Palais de Chaillot hosted an entire exhibit dedicated to Blake and Mortimer. Between 1997 and 1998, French children gobbled up the *Blake and Mortimer* cartoon, while in 2014 it was announced that the beloved duo would finally get a proper backstory in the form of a new comic strip. Thanks to British publisher Cinebook, English speakers in 2019 can enjoy old translations of the series and new editions, all of which are available on Amazon and other online retailers.

The enduring popularity of Blake and Mortimer is a timely reminder that readers in the West still hanker for proud imperial adventures featuring strong White male characters. Blake and Mortimer are not the chicken-chested weaklings that one finds dwelling in London or Brussels. Rather, these comic book heroes are reminiscent of the hardy men who settled the American West, the Pioneer Column that planted the Union Jack in Rhodesia, and everyday British warriors who fought two world wars in order to protect the empire. Francophone kids love Blake and Mortimer, and we should too. They are a fun reminder of our glorious past and an inspiration for our future.

---

[1] Tom Johnson, *Censored Screams: The British Ban on Hollywood Horror in the Thirties* (Jefferson, North Carolina and London: McFarland & Company, Inc.): p. 63–64.
[2] Claude le Gallo, *The World of Edgar P. Jacobs. In The Secret of the Swordfish, Part 3*, Edgar P. Jacobs, Trans. Jerome Saincantin (Canterbury, Kent: Cinebook Ltd, 2013): 58.
[3] Ian Mutsu, Introduction. In Edwin P. Hoyt, *Warlord: Tojo Against the World* (New York: Cooper Square Press, 2001): xviii.
[4] Hoyt, *Warlord*, 101–102.
[5] Fred L. Borch, *Military Trials of War Criminals in the Netherland East Indies, 1946–1949* (Oxford: Oxford University Press, 2017): 19–35.

KENYA'S NATIONAL HERO: A TERRORIST

American Renaissance, May 31st, 2019.

The closest thing to a national hero in Kenya is Dedan Kimathi. In addition to a giant and unattractive statue of him on Nairobi's Kimathi Street, his name adorns Nyeri's largest university. Kenyan men, especially those belonging to Kimathi's own Kikuyu tribe, are encouraged to be like the man who fought the British during the Mau Mau Rebellion of the 1950s.

The larger-than-life version of Kimathi—freedom fighter, intellectual, and martyr—is nowhere to be found in Ian Henderson and Philip Goodhart's *Man Hunt in Kenya*. Published in 1958, this slim, action-packed volume describes how Henderson and a handful of Europeans (mostly British men born in Kenya) turned Black, former anti-British terrorists into "pseudo-gangs" to destroy Kimathi's guerrilla network. When not describing the verdant splendor of British Kenya, Henderson describes Kimathi:

> *The British withdrawal from India had a profound effect on Kimathi, and he was also aware of the Egyptian terrorist activities in the Suez Canal Zone. He knew of the existence of the Soviet Union, but the theory of Communism and the subtleties of dialectical materialism meant nothing to him. He did, however, know the Bible as well as many lay preacher. . . . He spoke in parables, and his harangues were larded with allusions to and quotations from the Bible.[1]*

This may make Kimathi sound like any crazed street preacher, but he was the most vicious and powerful leader of the Mau Mau rebels. As a young man, Kimathi had imbibed the anti-White rhetoric of Jomo Kenyatta's Kenyan independence movement, plus Kimathi's version of Christianity saw him at the center as an African Christ. He also firmly believed in the ancient Kikuyu religion but did not respect tribal elders he considered subservient to the British. Kimathi took his rebellion to the mountains and forests, where he murdered several followers. It was the job of Henderson and his men to hunt him down.

Henderson was raised in the White Highlands of Kenya's Great Rift Valley. His family were Scottish immigrants, and his father Jock served with the British irregulars in the guerrilla war in German East Africa.[2] Ian inherited his father's rugged spirit, and he spent most of his youth tending the family's farm and exploring the lush forests around it. At age eighteen, as the Second World War was ending, he volunteered for the British Colonial Police. His physical fitness and knowledge of the Kikuyu language made him invaluable after the Mau Mau uprising broke out in earnest in 1950.

The origins of the Mau Mau movement are not entirely known, nor is its name clearly understood. In *Man Hunt in Kenya*, Henderson and Goodhart are convinced that the movement was either created or directed by Jomo Kenyatta and the Kenyan African National Union party.[3] Other historians rarely make this claim, but most want to blame all the violence on the British anyway. All observers do agree that the Mau Mau loathed the British and all White people and saw violence as the easiest way to gain independence for the Kikuyu.

The first members of the Mau Mau secret society were trade unionists and radical students from the cities of Nairobi and Nyeri. These militants moved into Kikuyu settlements and took part in oath swearing ceremonies that included animal fat and blood, promises to rid Kenya of Europeans, and allegiance to the Kikuyu god Ngai. To break this oath meant death. To oppose the Mau Mau or its goal of Black power in Kenya also meant death.

In 1952, Commissioner of Police Michael O'Rourke, a battle-tested veteran of the Palestine Police Force, became aware of new Kikuyu oath ceremonies in the Rift Valley and the Nairobi area that required adherents to be willing to kill Whites. The great paleo-anthropologist Louis Leakey, also a native of British East

Africa, heard Christian hymns sung at these ceremonies, though in praise of Kenyatta rather than Jesus.[4] White settlers mostly ignored these warning signs.

Many lived on lush farmlands in the central uplands, which became known as the White Highlands because non-White settlement was restricted. While the Happy Valley Set drank, took heroin, and fornicated in their well-maintained farmhouses, the Kikuyu majority of Kenya seethed with the type of indignation that comes from landlessness. Resentment boiled over in 1952.

At first the Mau Mau killed and disemboweled sheep and cows that belonged to European farmers. The first important murder was of Senior Chief Waruhiu Kungu, a Kikuyu chief the Mau Mau considered a traitor. Militants dressed as police officers gunned him down in his car seven miles outside of Nairobi, in an assassination that forced Governor Evelyn Baring to declare a state of emergency in the colony. This declaration meant British officials could start joint police and military operations, along with "villagization" campaigns, in which Kikuyus were put in detention camps.

The villagization campaign (which had been a great success against Communist insurgents in British Malaya) did not stop Mau Mau killings. On September 23rd and October 3rd, 1952, Mau Mau stabbed two British women to death at their farm near Thika.[5] In January 1953, approximately thirty Mau Mau killed the Ruck family—farmer Roger Ruck, his pregnant wife, and their six-year-old son—in their Rift Valley home. Newspapers reported that the family had been "slashed with pangas," a type of heavy knife favored by the Kikuyu. It later became known that the assailants took their time hacking up their victims. The Rucks ran a hospital for local Kikuyu.

Other European victims included an eighty-three-year-old who was clubbed to death, and Gray Leakey, the cousin of Louis Leakey. Gray was a fluent speaker of Kikuyu who had represented Jomo Kenyatta during a trial. Mau Mau entered the family home in North Nyeri, strangled Mrs. Mary Leakey, disemboweled the family's Kikuyu cook, and took Gray up into the forests of Mount Kenya. There they ate parts of his body and buried him alive upside down. [6] In total, the Mau Mau murdered thirty-two

Europeans, many more Asians (a majority of whom were Indians), and thousands of Africans. The worst Mau Mau atrocity was the murder of about one hundred Kikuyu, many of whom belonged to the pro-British Kikuyu Home Guard.

Chaos on this scale required more than a state of emergency. In late 1955, the police drew up a plan to capture and turn former Mau Mau terrorists into pro-government fighters. Known as pseudo-gangs, these former Mau Mau and their European officers went deep into the bush to track down small, often semi-independent Mau Mau groups. Henderson and his men excelled at this type of warfare. In *Man Hunt in Kenya*, Henderson describes the work it took to "flip" terrorists and turn them into allies.

Sometimes Kimathi himself made this easy because of his brutal leadership style. He beat or strangled anyone accused of spying for the British or of trying to seduce his wife. In other instances, Henderson on occasion leveraged Kikuyu superstition against Kimathi, who himself used witch doctors and the like to keep his soldiers in line. Much like the Simbas of a later war in the Congo, the Mau Mau fighters believed in omens, prophecy, and the promises of local conjure men who invoked the blessings of tribal gods before starting on military or cattle raids. So, knowing this, Henderson would sometimes talk to captured Mau Mau fighters about how Ngai favored the British. Henderson would back up this claim by pointing to successful bombing raids or adverse weather conditions that disrupted Kimathi's movements. Sometimes Kimathi did Henderson's work for him. Kimathi invoked bad omens and curses whenever his Mau Mau gang lost men or were forced to move for days on end because of British patrolling. When a curse was especially powerful, Kimathi demanded animal sacrifices.[7]

Henderson tried to draw Kimathi out of hiding in 1956 with coded letters left behind in Mau Mau mailboxes, which were nothing more than designated trees. When this failed, Henderson coated his face in shoe polish and burnt cork and tried approach Kimathi's gang. This failed too, for despite Henderson's fluency in the Kikuyu language, he and his fellow Europeans could not mask their features with black shoe polish. Also, captured Mau Mau fighters would later tell Henderson that the scent of soap gave away his position. Accordingly, Henderson and the Europeans went without bathing in the bush, and increasingly they let the pseudo-gangs take point on all patrols.

As for Kimathi, he grew increasingly paranoid. Near the end, in 1956, he spoke often to his few followers about strangling his wife and committing suicide on top of Mount Kenya. On October 21st, 1956, after Kimathi ran away from a British and Kenyan patrol, a member of the Kikuyu Home Guard shot him.[8] The British treated his wounds and put him on trial before an all-Black jury. It found him guilty, and on February 18th, 1957, Kimathi was hung inside the Kamiti Maximum Security Prison. No one knows where he is buried.

The man most responsible for bringing Kimathi to justice was far off in Nairobi on the day Kimathi was captured; Henderson and his wife were being introduced to Her Royal Highness, Princess Margaret, at a garden party.[9] Henderson continued to be the toast of Kenya (or at least White Kenya) until the nation became independent in 1962. The new Black government of Jomo Kenyatta deported him.

Although the British Empire was all but gone in 1962, Henderson still had the imperial dream. Rather than retreat to "Little England," he stayed abroad, and in 1966 was named the head of security for Bahrain. Henderson held this post until 1998 but earned the nickname "the Butcher" for supposedly authorizing the torture of political prisoners. He was a hero only from 1956 to 1957. For the rest of his life he was a villain: slayer of Kimathi and brutalizer of Gulf Arabs.

Many Blacks, including Nelson Mandela, who was himself a terrorist in the Kimathi mold, praise the Kenyan leader as an African Joan of Arc. In fact, he was something of a Trayvon Martin or a Michael Brown on a grander scale. He murdered far more Africans and Asians than Europeans and was bested by a farm boy-turned-police-officer.

[1] Henderson, Ian and Philip Goodhart, *Man Hunt in Kenya: The Termination of a Most Bizarre and Violent Terrorist Organization* (Toronto, New York, London, Sydney, Auckland: Bantam Books, 1988): 18.

[2] Henderson and Goodhart, *Man Hunt in Kenya*, 24.

[3] Henderson and Goodhart, *Man Hunt in Kenya*, 3.

[4] Van der Bijl, Nicholas, *The Mau Mau Rebellion: The Emergency in Kenya, 1952–1956* (Barnsley, South Yorkshire: Pen and Sword Military, 2017): 43.

[5] Van der Bijl, *The Mau Mau Rebellion*, 48.

[6] Anderson, David, *Histories of the Hanged: The Dirty War in Kenya and the End of Empire* (New York: W.W. Norton & Company, 2005): 117.

[7] Henderson and Goodhart, *Man Hunt in Kenya*, 173.

[8] Henderson and Goodhart, *Man Hunt in Kenya*, 227.

[9] Ibid.

White Giant: "Mad" Mike Hoare

Mike Hoare was a man out of time. Like his peer and fellow British Army veteran Colin Mitchell, Hoare earned the appellation "mad" because he seemed like a relic from the glory days of European imperialism. Hoare admitted that his ideals were out-of-step in his own account of his days in the Congo much in the same way that "Mad" Mitch mockingly labeled himself a "nigger-bashing imperialist." However, while both men shared a fondness for lost causes and the same Celtic temperament, "Mad" Mitch always seemed far more theatrical than "Mad" Mike. After all, only someone with a flair for the dramatic would constantly pepper the streets of Aden, an Arab metropolis, with the sounds of Scottish bagpipes.

Hoare, who had his own Scottish piper, is best known for his time serving as the leader of 5 Commando—a group of mercenaries who fought during the last days of the Congo Crisis between 1963 and 1965. *Congo Mercenary*, Hoare's very readable account of 5 Commando's war, served as the inspiration for the hit 1978 film, *The Wild Geese*. The White mercenaries in the film are slightly more romantic, if not more roughish than Hoare's men. After all, *Congo Mercenary* makes it all too clear why men from South Africa, Rhodesia, West Germany, and Italy signed up for 5 Commando:

> *Much as I would like to say that we were motivated by anti-communist sentiments I am unable, in truth, to say so. Here and there, there may have been an idealist whose actions were governed by these principles, as there were also some who came for adventure and not basically the reward, but by and large we were there for one reason only—money. Having accepted the mercenary calling the*

only principle I insisted upon was a reasonable standard of personal behavior.[1]

For Hoare, the gold standard of soldiering (or at least mercenary soldiering) became the symbol of 5 Commando—the image of the Wild Goose, which meant to symbolize 5 Commando's inheritance from the 19,000 Irish mercenaries who served as the "Wild Geese" for the Catholic kingdoms of Europe in the eighteenth century. Hoare, the son of an Irish family with a long military tradition, certainly knew his history. *Congo Mercenary* also shows that Hoare was an astute observer of geopolitics, sociology, and race. Indeed, those inclined towards the Dissident Right might label Hoare an early "race realist." He certainly made no bones in his writings about what could cure Congo and all sub-Saharan Africa after the colonial powers left.

> *"The effects of the too hasty independence have certainly been far reaching and calamitous, but it is no too late to make amends. The salvation of the Congo, as I see it, will be the reintroduction of as many Europeans as are prepared to emigrate to the country to become the fabric of the Congo, to help the Congolese on the road to political maturity and to teach them the skills of commerce and administration.[2]*

Hoare, like Ian Smith of Rhodesia, sincerely believed that White civilization could bring Black Africa out of its generational malaise. However, both men believed that native Africans had their limits, and *Congo Mercenary* is unflinching when it comes to detailing the savagery of Afro-Marxists and Black Nationalists once they recognized that the Europeans had pulled out of Africa.

In order to understand the full extent of Hoare's commentary, as well as the heroic feats that his men pulled off, one has to understand the unique history of the Congo and where the country stood just after achieving independence.

The Heart of Darkness

Thanks to Adam Hochschild's critically praised book *King Leopold's Ghost,* Congo's colonial past has become synonymous with racial genocide. According to Hochschild's account, King Leopold II, who created the Congo Free State as a "personal union" (essentially, the Congo was Leopold's private property), turned the largest African nation into a giant sweatshop. Here, capitalist enterprise and the cultivation of rubber forced millions of native Congolese to toil for little to no wages at all. If they rebelled or shirked their duties, King Leopold's representatives would cut off their hands. Worse still, Hochschild argues that Leopold oversaw a massive campaign of genocide that killed ten million people.

The only problem with this number is that it is fabricated. Ryan Faulk pointed out with great clarity that the best estimate of the Congolese population in 1885 was only 9,801,150 people. That population rose by 1900. Furthermore, the European council that ultimately removed King Leopold from power in the Congo could find no conclusive documentation that official policy dictated amputations as punishment. Faulk notes that even outraged Europeans who considered Leopold a butcher concluded that most of these amputations were done by poorly disciplined members of the *Force Publique*, the local army made up of Black troops and White officers. Historian Barbara Emerson and others have called out Hochschild for his lazy research and broad assumptions. Hochschild's personal history (and early life) as a Boomer veteran of the anti-war movement and various far-left publications (*Mother Jones, Ramparts*) makes it obvious that his depiction of King Leopold II is based on political expediency and personal interst. Another bad European male is good for business, you see.

In 1908, the government of Belgium officially took control of the Congo. The small half-French, half-Dutch nation found itself as the ruler of the richest prize in all of Africa. However, Roger Anstey argues in his 1966 book *King Leopold's Legacy* that Brussels looked on its good fortune with trepidation. Anstey, no apologist for Belgian colonialism, notes that "Belgium's position in 1908, in regard to the Congo, was akin to that of an heir who inherits an estate with a predominating sense of duty, rather than fulfillment of a long-felt wish."[3] Still, despite misgivings, Brussels turned the Congo into a powerful colony. The *Force Publique* was one of the best-trained armies in all colonial Africa, and even scored victories in World War I over the brilliant German general Paul von Lettow-Vorbeck. Belgian technicians helped to build beautiful cities like Leopoldville, Stanleyville, and Elizabethville. Hoare, a proud citizen of Her Majesty's realm, admitted that Belgium surpassed all other European powers in terms of construction and investment in their colony.

> [I]n my journeying around the Congo I had seen with my own eyes ample evidence of an enormous Belgian investment in the country, both in money and labour. Beautiful towns and cities with prosperous and thriving industries had been won from the suffocating equatorial jungle. Magnificent schools and missions had arisen, where once there had been nothing but disease and pestilence. Every village now boasted its own clinic. No village was so humble but it possessed its own water pump. . . .[4]

Raw economic statistics reveal the truth behind Hoare's words. According to Howard Epstein's thoroughly detailed history of Congo's first years of independence, "in the years just before independence the Belgian Congo had become the most developed country in tropical Africa."[5] Between the years of 1950 and 1957, the Belgian Congo enjoyed an impressive annual growth rate of 6.7 percent. By 1959, the Belgian Congo had a commercial surplus of $192 million. The country enjoyed the highest wages and literacy rates in all sub-Saharan Africa.[6] These are not indicators of a country in decline or in need of a massive socio-political revolution.

That happened anyway in 1960. On May 22nd, the Congolese National Movement became the largest and most powerful party in the Congo. The party's leader, Patrice Lumumba, came from the educated middle class of the country. He sought guidance from the liberal Enlightenment, with Rousseau and Voltaire as his chief heroes. The Belgian state considered him a secret "red" and a criminal (the latter charge was true—Lumumba was arrested in Belgium for embezzlement in 1956). During his short reign in 1960, Lumumba positioned himself as a radical Black Nationalist and potential friend of the Communists in Moscow and Beijing. Although he paid lip service to the idea that Whites had helped to bring about Congolese independence, Lumumba's followers were often motivated by fanatical race hatred and superstition. This fact would later require the services of "Mad" Mike Hoare and his 5 Commando.

In the interim, Congolese independence became something of a sham almost immediately. In Leopoldville, Lumumba tried to establish a centralized state against the wishes of more federalist-minded Congolese politicians. Chief among this latter group was Moise Tshombe. Tshombe and his CONAKAT (roughly, the Confederation of Associated Tribes of Katanga) party declared the southern state of Katanga independent. Lumumba and his supporters could not stomach this secession, for Katanga was the economic dynamo of the entire country. Katanga was well-known for its copper mines, abundant plantations, and large cobalt and diamond reserves. Even worse for Lumumba, Tshombe, a Christian and a member of the Lunda tribe, sought to keep close relations with Belgium and the West to present a united anti-communist front in Africa.

The United Nations and the United States gave their support to Lumumba. In large part that was due to America's anti-colonial policy. On the other hand, Lumumba was undeniably popular with Black people across the globe. He even popularized the notion that America's prestige and wealth came only because of Black labor. "Africans built America and developed America," Lumumba told a crowd in Stanleyville in 1960. "They are the reason that America has become a great world power."[7] For an America during a Civil Rights revolution, officially condemning Lumumba was seen as a furtherance of "White supremacist" politics. Even in 1960, the fear of being branded as "racist" trumped the fact that the US knew full well that Lumumba's government had formerly requested Soviet and Chinese aid, even including a July 14th, 1960 letter that asked for a military intervention from Moscow in case of a Belgian "conspiracy" against Congolese independence.[8]

In 1960, UN troops were sent to the Congo to prop up the weak central state. Even this move proved controversial, as several Afro-Marxist states, including Ghana and Uganda, felt that the UN should only send Black African troops to the Congo rather than the Indian, Moroccan, Irish, and Swedish troops that they actually sent. The Whites of the Congo supported Tshombe to the point where they occasionally took up arms against UN "peacekeepers." The famous Siege of Jadotville (1961) should be rightly remembered as a story of Irish heroism, but it should not be overlooked that those Irish troops were fighting on behalf of a Congolese government that not only tried to force Katanga into an unwanted union, but also sought to further Lumumba's legacy—a legacy that Tshombe, Congo's White citizens, and several tribes found toxic.

Lumumba's arrest and execution in 1961 put some of the thornier issues to rest. An international commission created in 1961 found that Lumumba's execution had been ordered by Tshombe and carried out by members of Katanga's gendarmerie. Many left-wing academics believe that Lumumba was executed by the CIA, Britain's MI6, and other Western spooks. Whatever the case, Lumumba became a martyr.

This martyrdom would help to foment a serious revolution in 1964. Called the Simba Rebellion, this violent outbreak bore many disturbing similarities to the military mutinies that initiated Congolese independence four years prior. In 1960, members of the military and rival tribes began rampaging through the cities of Leopoldville and Luluabourg. Not too long afterwards, their public displays of violence took on a racial character, with Congolese troops abducting, raping, and murdering White citizens. Thousands of White citizens fled the country or to Katanga, where President Tshombe promised protection. The riots of 1960 proved so bad that 800 Belgian paratroopers, at the request of President Tshombe, returned to Elizabethville to put down a mutiny that had already killed six Whites.[9] Belgian troops would stay in the country until African protests grew too loud, and the UN forced them to leave.

White Giants Arrive

By 1964, the Belgian presence in the Congo had dwindled considerably. Belgian military officers still served as advisors to the Congolese army, but that was about it. Unfortunately, despite the presence of Belgian officers, the Congolese army proved totally incapable of putting down a small, pro-Communist rebellion that erupted in Kwilu Province. Because of this inefficiency, and because the rebels received unchecked aid from Uganda and the Sudan, the rebellion conquered two-thirds of the nation in just five months.[10] Despite this civil war, UN troops continued to leave the country because of an early security agreement with Leopoldville. Knowing full well that the Congo hung precariously close to dissolution, President Joseph Kasavubu named Tshombe as the country's new Prime Minister. Tshombe received nearly unlimited powers, and he used these powers to immediately order the creation of mercenary units to augment the failing Congolese army. This move immediately earned Tshombe the ire of both the African communists and international organizations such as the UN and the OAU (an organization of Francophone countries in Africa). From his home in Durban, South Africa, Hoare got the call to head 5 Commando. Tshombe promised him unfettered control over his men, their pay, and deployment. He would receive none of this, and his men almost mutinied several times because of lack of pay.

Hoare had first cut his teeth as a member of the London Irish Rifles in World War II. During the war, he served in India (his birthplace) and Burma, where he got a first-hand look at the long-range reconnaissance tactics of the Chindits. The Chindits utilized light infantry tactics and highly mobile warfare to harass the Japanese and their local allies in Southeast and Southern Asia. Such techniques would become the trademark of 5 Commando. By the time President Tshombe gave Hoare the green light to establish a thousand-man mercenary army in the Congo, the fighting Irishman had already served in Katanga as a member of Tshombe's police force.

Hoare began looking for volunteers by placing this simple advertisement in the newspapers of Johannesburg and Salisbury:

Any fit young man looking for employment with a difference at a salary well in excess of 100 pounds per month should telephone 838-5203 during business hours. Employment initially offered for six months. Immediate start.[11]

Volunteers for Hoare's 5 Commando mostly came from South Africa and Rhodesia, those White African countries most threatened by a Communist takeover in the Congo. Other volunteers came from Greece, Italy, and the Portuguese colonies of Mozambique and Angola. British, Canadian, and American volunteers joined too, and so did German, Belgian, and French soldiers. 5 Commando's air force was made up entirely of Cuban expats who loathed Communism because of their experiences with Fidel Castro. Some of Hoare's men lived up to the sordid reputation of mercenaries, with standout troopers including a Dane who boiled African skulls to sell to international buyers and one professional soccer player who raped and murdered a local woman after she mocked the size of his penis. German journalist Hans Germani, who joined as a rifle-carrying medic, described other interesting characters who wound up in 5 Commando.

For instance, Charles Gardien, a mercenary veteran of Egypt's war in North Yemen, went to Congo to fight Communism. Gardien's anti-Communism was coupled with a fondness for Black women, according to Germani. Other odd characters included a Rhodesian-born lieutenant named Paul Galinos, an Austrian mechanic named Ingo Hudovernik, a wealthy Belgian jeweler named Leon de Grouwe, a former French Foreign Legion soldier named Edward Lambrette, and a Belgian White supremacist with connections to the OAS named Jungels.[12] In his own account, Hoare plays down the eccentricities of his men in favor of lauding their excellent soldiering skills, their bravery, and, at times, their idealism. Both Germani and Hoare spent copious pages detailing the softness of these hated White mercenaries. Even Jungels is shown carrying a young Black child to safety.

These are the men that the Simba rebels called "white giants."

The humanity of the commandos contrasted drastically with the utter savagery of the rebels. Both Hoare and Germani described the rebellious Simbas ("young lions") as drug-fueled adolescents with a license to kill. Their leaders, like Gaston Soumialot, were committed Communists, but most Simbas cared only about revenge against the Congo's Whites and the chance to rape and pillage to their heart's content.[13] For them, Lumumba was both a warrior for the Black race and a powerful wizard. *Congo Mercenary* details how tribal witch doctors, even some who claimed to be Christian, would convince the rebel soldiers that their magic could help to turn bullets into water. The power of local witchcraft could be comical (such as when rebels would shout incantations in order to protect themselves from bombs and FAL rounds), but in the case of the Congo in 1964, it was mostly malevolent.

Stanleyville and the War for Civilization

The most infamous moment of the entire Simba Rebellion occurred when the city of Stanleyville fell on August 4th, 1964. Thanks to sixty trucks containing rebel soldiers and witch doctors, the entire Congolese army garrison in the city gave up and ran away without a fight. A day later, the rebels controlled the Stanleyville Airport. With the city on lockdown, the large White population was fair game.

Hoare's 5 Commando, which included several inexperienced and ill-trained volunteers, rushed into action immediately and set about liberating towns and villages along the approach to Stanleyville. After taking the village of Kindu, which had been subjected to the devious desires of one fourteen-year-old rebel, 5 Commando learned the true horror of the rebellion.

A young boy of about fourteen had installed himself as the chief executioner, and took fiendish delight in running up and down the line hacking his panga [a machete-like tool] at a defenceless man here, or savagely attacking a woman there, lopping off a hand or a foot as it took his fancy. The crowd would encourage him in his excesses, until maddened with his own power he would give the order to fire, when a dozen or more Simbas would open up at point-blank range, sometimes killing, sometimes wounding the men and women selected for death that day. The bodies of the prisoners were then flung into the Lualaba, dead or alive.[14]

European and American nuns and priests provided the rebels with their favorite targets. Even professional airmen were not exempt from slaughter. Three years earlier, in 1961, mutinous soldiers had captured nineteen Italian air force pilots. These men were tortured, murdered, and partially eaten by their captors. The rest of their body parts wound up as meat in small markets in rebel territory.[15] Most of these outrages would occur in front of shrines or monuments to Lumumba, who became a kind of anti-White fetish for the rebels. Germani summed up their relationship to Lumumba and his ideals: "it was a fanatic movement against the White man, an appeal to wild dreams of a coloured dominion of the world."[16] Germani and Hoare both agreed that the rebellion of 1964 represented an atavistic revolt with just a patina of orthodox Communism at the very top.

The rebels of 1964 also proved that death can sometimes be preferable. Both Hoare and Germani recounted stories of European and American nuns who were raped every day for months by rebels. Some of these victims became pregnant, and upon being liberated by the mercenaries, had to deal with the issue of getting an abortion—a cardinal sin in the Catholic Church. Others, including both men and women, were forced to eat the excrement of rebels while local villages watched and laughed. More than a few White civilians saw their husbands, wives, and children murdered before their eyes. *Congo Mercenary* shows that rebel warlords often tried to make young White girls their concubines. When they resisted, they were often killed outright. As the war dragged on and the rebels increasingly lost ground, revolutionary officers gave orders to kill every White person within in striking distance. Such an order was carried out in the small town of Likati, where an entire Greek family, including two infants, were killed by Simbas.[17]

At Stanleyville, between November 24th and 27th, approximately seventeen White hostages faced the threat of death at the hands of rebels under the command of Christopher Gbenye, a protégé of Lumumba. Gbenye refused to let the International Red Cross into the city, and he refused to let anyone leave. This forced Brussels to intervene with Operation Dragon Rogue, a multi-national operation featuring Belgian paratroopers descending on the city after jumping out of American planes. 5 Commando stood outside of the city until given the go-ahead by Belgian military advisors. Hoare's men would eventually enter the city but were too late to stop the murder of those White civilians who had been held prisoner at Stanleyville's formerly posh Hotel Victoria.

On the morning when 5 Commando raced towards the city, Gbenye's official newspaper and radio station belched out: "Ciyuga, Ciyuga! Kill, kill! Kill all the White people. Kill all the men, women, and children. Kill them all. Have no scruples. Use your knives and your pangas!" [18] When the mostly Belgian and American hostages were eviscerated, Belgian paratroopers were just two miles away and 5 Commando's jeeps and trucks were racing towards the heart of the city. The European owner of the once prestigious Stanleyville Hotel summed up the terrible trauma of the city's White population when he told marauding soldiers to drink up everything in the hotel bar. As for him, he was going back to Belgium and leaving the "God-forsaken" Congo.[19]

The Secret History

Despite the well-documented cruelties of Stanleyville and other unknown villages throughout the Congo, the Western press continued to write biased articles in favor of the rebels. One West German periodical even wrote with a straight face that "the Rebels kept order; they always swept the streets clean." [20] As for the mercenaries, they always got bad press, with European and American reporters telling lurid tales about mercenary atrocities and runaway looting (Hoare is not shy about admitting that, at times, his men indulged in taking booty). Such partisan tactics would have a much greater impact during America's war in Vietnam.

Another German journalist, Uwe Siemon-Netto, would write decades later that "media celebrities of a new kind and their youthful wannabe acolytes" went to Vietnam as the "products of increasingly ideological liberal arts colleges and universities."[21] These same political operatives used their skills as agitprop artists to great effect during the Tet Offensive, a military disaster for the North Vietnamese that turned into a propaganda victory thanks to skewed reporting and millions of eager anti-war protestors. At the Battle of Hue, Siemon-Netto saw left-wing reporters try to convince themselves that the victims of North Vietnamese death squads had been killed by American bombers. [22] Such bias undoubtedly colored their reporting.

For 5 Commando, they realized that the world, especially the West, did not want to know that the Simba rebels carried out their massacres thanks to Chinese guns, Ugandan mercenaries, and Cuban and Algerian trainers. By 1965, during 5 Commando's final push into the border lands that connect the Congo with Sudan and Uganda, Hoare's men not only found that Simbas would retreat across the border into Uganda when things got too hot, but also that reports written in Spanish kept appearing at abandoned Simba outposts. Evidence also showed that Algerian soldiers were on the ground in the Congo, and they showed the Simbas how to use and detonate lethal mines that had earlier worked against the French.

The war in the Congo, which so often is portrayed in the American classroom as a neocolonial affair, was actually part of the Cold War, where anti-White, Afro-Marxist forces received direct aid from the communist world while pro-Western forces got terribly little from either Europe or America.

Tragically, Hoare and 5 Commando became victims of their own success. As the war reached its final days in late 1965, President Tshombe was removed from office by a political rival. This created a political crisis that forced yet another military coup in the young nation. Unfortunately, the wheels had already been set for a closer collaboration between Leopoldville and Brazzaville, the capital of the Republic of the Congo. This allowed left-wing agitators from Brazzaville to enter the Democratic Republic of the Congo and foment further political unrest. Even before 5 Commando had completed the destruction of the last Simba redoubts, left-wing protestors ransacked Leopoldville, burned the Belgian flag, and defiled a statue of King Leopold II. [23] The politicians of Leopoldville furthered this blunder by cancelling Hoare's contract and disbanding 5 Commando. Germani called this the destruction of the "white giants" by the "white dwarfs."

Whatever the truth, it cannot be denied that "Mad" Mike Hoare and 5 Commando stopped a possible genocide in the making. This small band of mercenaries momentarily saved the Congo from itself through sheer bravery and excellent soldiering. *Congo Mercenary* deliberately tries to compare 5 Commando to the past heroics of White men in Africa, like the British explorer Henry Morton Stanley, British engineer Cecil Rhodes, and British scout Allan Wilson, who led the insanely brave Shangani Patrol during the First Matabele War. Even in 1965, when there still existed European colonies in Africa, such comparisons were hopelessly old fashioned. 5 Commando perished along with the last flames of imperial adventure in the "Dark Continent."

In spite of the dismal situation in the Congo and the fact that the nation has been mired in constant warfare since 1996, the accomplishments of Hoare and his men deserve to be recognized for the contribution they made to Congolese society and history. Hoare, his mercenaries, and those Belgian advisors who stayed on in the Congo all shed their sweat and blood to maintain the Congo as the most civilized and economically powerful nation in equatorial Africa. They succeeded, but their victories were discarded like waste by cowardly politicians.

All the problems of the Congo today are the fault of the Congolese and the Congolese government. "Mad" Mike Hoare recognized this as early as 1967, and it still holds true today.

[1] Hoare, Mike. *Congo Mercenary* (London: Robert Hale, 1967): 68.
[2] Ibid, 285.
[3] Anstey, Roger. *King Leopold's Legacy: The Congo Under Belgian Rule, 1908–1960* (London, New York, and Ibadan: Oxford University Press, 1966): 37.
[4] Hoare, 283.
[5] Epstein, Howard M., Ed. *Revolt in the Congo, 1960–1964* (New York: Facts on File, 1965): 176.
[6] Ibid, 177.
[7] Epstein, 35.
[8] Ibid, 17.
[9] Ibid, 10.
[10] Hoare, 13.
[11] Ibid, 33.
[12] Germani, Hans. *White Soldiers in Black Africa* (Beperk: Nasionale Boekhandel, 1967): 12–13.
[13] Ibid, 4.
[14] Hoare, 91.
[15] Germani, 30.
[16] Ibid, 57.
[17] Hoare, 233–234.
[18] Ibid, 121–122.
[19] Ibid, 129.
[20] Germani, 37.
[21] Siemon-Netto, Uwe. *Duc: A Reporter's Love for the Wounded People of Vietnam* (Self-Published, 2013): 74.
[22] Ibid, 199.
[23] Hoare, 278.

JOCK'S LAW:
"MAD MITCH" AND BRITAIN'S LAST DAYS IN ADEN

Ian Fleming's James Bond novels provide an excellent glimpse into the mind of a British Tory during the last days of the British Empire. In *You Only Live Twice*, Tiger Tanaka, a member of the Japanese secret service, crudely criticizes Bond's beloved England by taunting: "Britain has not only lost a great Empire, you have seemed almost anxious to throw it away with both hands." Bond responds weakly, saying[1]:

> *England may have been bled pretty thin by a couple of world wars. . . . But there's nothing wrong with the British people – although there are only fifty million of them.*

Bond's patriotism is commendable. It is the same type of patriotism that Fleming supported in his interview with *Playboy* magazine in 1964:

> *I am British, and proud of being British, and I'm not going to dodge fair payment by making a dash for Switzerland or one of the other tax paradises.*

Tax chauvinism—that is all the proud British man has left. Without question, even Bond recognizes that his Britain won World War II, but wound up losing its empire anyway. Tanaka, as a member of the Japanese elite, reminds Bond and Fleming's readers both that the defeated Japanese came out of the late 1940s smelling like roses. Great Britain, on the other hand, volunteered for socialist state planning that wrecked its economy for decades.

The Imperial Tory complaint implicit in the Bond novels found a real world parallel in the life of Lieutenant Colonel Colin Mitchell.

A Londoner by birth, but a Scotsman by blood, Mitchell was only truly loyal to the Argyll and Sutherland Highlanders. This had been his father's regiment, and in 1944, it became Mitchell's regiment as well.

World War II represented the last great gasp of Britain's Imperial Army. The outnumbered army that faced down 12,000 Japanese at Kohima and killed 6,000 of them[2] would later be the same army that handed over Kenya to Black Nationalists after defeating the Mau Mau insurgents on the ground.[3] Much like their contemporaries in the American military fighting against Communism in Vietnam, Cambodia, and Laos, British military commanders, especially junior officers, complained that their government was forcing them to fight rearguard actions with one hand tied behind their backs. Prime Minister Clement Attlee, the Labour PM who created Britain's modern welfare state, led the charge for the dissolution of the British Empire when he granted India independence in 1947.

There is this immense nation, set in the midst of Asia, an Asia which has been ravaged by war. Here we have the one great country that has been seeking to apply the principles of democracy. I have always hoped myself that politically India might be the light of Asia.[4]

Labour had long agitated for the fall or at least the shrinking of the British Empire. When their wish came true in South Asia, it set off a series of genocidal conflicts that may have killed as many as two million people and displaced fifteen million more.[5]

Undeterred, the Conservative government of Prime Minister Harold Macmillan put their wet thumbs in the air and felt the winds of change blowing in British Africa. In 1960, Macmillan told the British people that:

The wind of change is blowing through this continent, and whether we like it or not, this growth of national consciousness is a political fact. We must all accept it as a fact, and our national policies must take account of it.

Macmillan's speech not only signaled that Britain was abandoning its international standing in the face of Soviet and American pressure, but it also told the White minority governments of South Africa and Rhodesia that the defense of Western values in Africa would be left up to them and them only. Today, those Western values are buried under unimaginably high crime statistics, corruption, and an endemic culture of anti-European hatred.

By 1966, one of the last outposts of British culture abroad was the port city of Aden. This would not last much longer, for in that year, the Labour government of Harold Wilson, working under the influence of Soviet and Egyptian agents, announced that British troops would be leaving the city by the end of 1967. Mitchell's beloved Argyll and Sutherland Highlanders would be the last British soldiers to be sent into Aden.

At the time, London belonged to Harold Wilson, an Oxford-educated economist and former member of the Liberal Party. According to Peter Hitchens in *The Broken Compass*, the Wilson government of 1964–1970 "began and consolidated the cultural and moral revolution, turned the schools into egalitarian engines, and transformed the welfare state from a safety net into a powerful disincentive to unskilled work." Wilson's government is the same one that bankrupted the British economy by devaluing the pound in 1967. In the midst of declining manufacturing, Wilson defended his decision by trying to argue that devaluation would get at the "root cause" of wealth inequality in the country.[6] The exchange rate dropped from $2.80 to $2.40, a difference of about 14 percent.

If Wilson represented the new technocratic elite of post-imperial Britain, then Mitchell represented the old guard of the empire. Mitchell, in the words of Ioan Grillo, embodied the "adventuring upper-class officers" that provided so many of the British Empire's best men.[7] Put in my blunt language, Mitchell jokingly referred to himself as a "nigger-bashing imperialist" as a way to contrast himself with the more modern British Army officers who saw their jobs as an extension of the civil service.

Mitchell cut his teeth in the infantry campaign of the Argenta Gap in April 1945. From there, Mitchell had combat stints in Kenya, Malaya, Korea, and Borneo, the latter of which involved a technically unofficial British attempt to keep Indonesia from occupying Malaysia. His time serving in Palestine, which today still stands as the deadliest engagement for British troops since the end of World War II,[8] added to Mitchell's legend. Namely, he survived the Irgun's bombing of Jerusalem's King David Hotel through a stroke of sheer luck.

More importantly, the Lt. Col. Mitchell who was sent to Aden was an experienced hand in counterinsurgency warfare. He had fought Somali guerrillas alongside the newly created Kenyan Army; he had fought both Arab and Jewish insurgents in Mandatory Palestine; he had tried to keep the peace in Zanzibar when Arab and African citizens tried to massacre one another. More importantly, Mitchell had dealt with the EOKA insurgency in Cyprus. The Cyprus Emergency saw British troops employing the same successful tactics they utilized against the Chinese Communists of Malaya, but it also saw British junior officers dismantle an ethno-political terrorist group that targeted British officials for assassination.[9]

In Aden, the National Liberation Front (NLF) and the Front for the Liberation of Occupied South Yemen (FLOSY) controlled the streets. These two groups attracted the "detribalized" men of Aden, many of whom regularly listened to Cairo Radio, an engine of Arab Marxism that Egypt's Gamal Abdul Nasser used in order to propagate anti-Western ideas throughout the Arab world. The "Arabists" in the British Army did not trust the Adeni at all. To the British, the Adeni were "Loafers" and "Suk Rats." Unfortunately, the Labour government identified themselves with the nationalists of Aden, many of whom represented left-wing labor unions. This led to a permanent freeze on British combat operations in Aden. British troops were supposed to quietly train their replacements (the South Arabian Army) then leave the city to its fate. FLOSY and NLF had other ideas.

Beginning in 1961, these two groups began a reign of terror that targeted not only the British Army and their Arab supporters, but also British civilians. On December 10th, 1963, an NLF grenade attack on British high commissioner Sir Kennedy Trevaskis killed two and wounded twenty-four. A more infamous grenade attack occurred on December 23rd, 1964, when an NLF terrorist threw a grenade into a Christmas party hosted by a Royal Air Force officer.[10] A sixteen-year-old girl died in the attack. All told, the British officials in Aden recorded 3,710 terrorist "incidents" between 1964 and 1967.[11]

Despite this, the British Army maintained a passive status quo. This only changed on June 19th, 1967. On that day, FLOSY and NLF agents within the British-trained Aden Armed Police mutinied and killed twenty-two members of the King's Own Royal Border Regiment, the Royal Northumbrian Fusiliers, and Lancashire Regiment. Most of the casualties came when NLF/FLOSY gunmen surprised a convoy of British troops in armored cars. With their own men lying dead in the middle of the Crater district of Aden, the British brass decided to pull back and leave that district to the terrorists. Even the British tanks in Aden received stand-down orders. A weak curfew was called, SAS agents entered the Crater, and snipers ringed along the hills overlooking the city traded shots with insurgents. Other than these tepid measures, the British fully abandoned the Crater.

Lt. Col. Mitchell saw this cowardice firsthand. The Argyll and Sutherland Highlanders were due to take control of the remaining British outposts in the city just a few days later, so Mitchell was shadowing the Royal Northumberland Fusiliers when the mutiny broke out. Mitchell decided upon a completely different tact when it came time for his men to walk the streets of Aden.

"I took flamboyant risks in order to demonstrate to my own officers and NCOs that we led from the front," Mitchell would later say about his leadership style in the summer of 1967. These "flamboyant risks" included telling a Scottish bagpiper to play "Monymusk" on July 3rd. On that same night, the Argyll and Sutherland Highlanders walked into the Crater without losing a man. Mitchell called this moment and the playing of the bagpipes "the most thrilling sound in the world."

It stirs the blood and reminds one of the heritage of Scotland and the Regiment. Best of all it frightens the enemy to death.

Mitchell, whom the British press dubbed "Mad Mitch" because of his flagrant disregard for the orders handed down by his superiors, further demoralized his Arab enemies by unleashing the full wrath of his soldiers. This became colloquially known as "Jock's Law," a type of tribal warfare where the Argyll and Sutherland Highlanders acted more like conquerors than a regiment on the eve of leaving for good. The Jocks (the Scottish version of "Tommy") became a law onto themselves—they beat suspected terrorists out in the open or pummeled them into submission at their regiment's headquarters in the Crater. Some of these Jocks stole money from the Adeni, whom they considered dirty "wogs." Much of this brutality was captured on camera, and to the surprise of the Wilson government, the British public loved it. The birth of "Jock's Law" in Aden made "Mad Mitch" a hero.

Mitchell, whom later historians have characterized as a "surreal relic of Britain's colonial past: a crazed fusion of the Celtic madman, belligerent imperialist and cantankerous military commander," [12] angered the British establishment because he thumbed his nose at the idea that London should gracefully bow out of the world stage. Although the British Army punished Mitchell for his success in Aden by making a promotion impossible, "Mad Mitch" ultimately proved to the world that pure violence can be more effective in controlling unruly populations than the velvet glove treatment. The Jocks of Mitchell's regiment also proved the power of tribal thinking. Unlike their predecessors, the Scottish soldiers of the Argyll and Sutherland Highlanders effectively pacified FLOSY and NLF because they thought and fought more like a clan army than the rule-bound soldiers of a neoliberal state.

---

[1] Benjamin Welton, "Born on the Brink: The Birth of James Bond and the Decline of the British Empire," *Artistic License Renewed*, Oct. 29, 2014, https://literary007.com/2014/10/29/born-on-the-brink-the-birth-of-james-bond-and-the-decline-of-the-british-empire/.
[2] Richard Holmes, "Ten of the greatest classic British Army victories," *Daily Telegraph*, Jan. 23, 2010, https://www.dailymail.co.uk/home/moslive/article-1244764/Ten-greatest-classic-British-Army-victories.html.
[3] "Mau Mau uprising: Bloody history of Kenya conflict, *BBC.com*, Apr. 7, 2011, https://www.bbc.com/news/uk-12997138.
[4] Address given by Clement Attlee to the House of Commons, Mar. 15, 1946.

[5] William Dalrymple, "The Great Divide," *The New Yorker*, Jun. 22, 2015.

[6] "1967: Wilson defends 'pound in your pocket,'" *BBC.com*, http://news.bbc.co.uk/onthisday/hi/dates/stories/november/19/newsid_3208000/3208396.stm.

[7] Ion Grillo, *El Narco: Inside Mexico's Criminal Insurgency* (New York: Bloomsbury, 2012): 95–96.

[8] "In Memoriam - the 784 (at least) left behind," *British Forces in Palestine*, Aug. 2018, http://www.britishforcesinpalestine.org/inmemoriam.html.

[9] Dr. Andrekos Varnava, Review of *Fighting EOKA: The British Counter-Insurgency Campaign on Cyprus, 1955–1959* by David French, *Reviews in History*, https://reviews.history.ac.uk/review/1901.

[10] Charles Messenger, *For Love of Regiment: A History of British Infantry, Volume 2, 1915–1994* (London: Leo Cooper, 1996): 184

[11] Nicholas van der Bijl, *British Military Operations in Aden and Radfan: 100 Years of British Colonial Rule* (Barnsley, South Yorkshire: Pen and Sword Military, 2014): Kindle edition.

[12] Fred Halliday, *Arabia Without Sultans* (London: Saqi, 2013): Kindle edition.

American Renaissance, March 12th, 2018.

The story of Rhodesia has a strong resonance with "red pilled" White Americans. Since Rhodesia is now Zimbabwe, it is not a happy story. Indeed, Rhodesia shows us what can happen when Whites become a powerless minority. In 1980, Rhodesia, once the "breadbasket of Africa," began its steep decline into the worst economic disaster in human history.

However, the story of Rhodesia is not all doom and gloom. This little White-minority nation stood up to the world, and despite a massive economic embargo that lasted for over a decade, Rhodesia managed to hang on and win victory after victory on the battlefield. 1977's Operation Dingo is a testament to the strength, endurance, and ingenuity of the small but professional Rhodesian Security Forces. British General Sir Walter Walker, upon reviewing Operation Dingo, said of the Rhodesian fighting man:

> *Their army cannot be defeated in the field either by terrorists or even a much more sophisticated enemy. In my professional judgement based on more than twenty years' experience from lieutenant to general, of counter-insurgency and guerilla-type operations, there is no doubt that Rhodesia now has the most professional and battle-worthy army in the world for this particular type of warfare.[1]*

Although a vast majority of the men who served in famous outfits like the Rhodesian SAS, the Selous Scouts, and the Rhodesian Light Infantry, were sons of Rhodesian soil, the country did welcome foreign mercenaries during the long Bush War of the

1960s and 1970s. Most of these mercenaries went to White Africa thanks to advertisements in *Soldier of Fortune* magazine. A large portion also came from South Africa, where Anglo and Boer Whites have a long tradition of serving as soldiers-for-hire. Do not forget that Rhodesia itself was established by mercenaries in the employ of visionary elitist and devout imperialist Cecil Rhodes. His British South Africa Company hired the best trackers and settlers of British Africa in order turn the Bantu lands of the Limpopo River into Rhodesia.

One mercenary group during the Bush War, the "Crippled Eagles," won a modicum of fame because its members came from the United States. Veterans of this unique outfit included several Vietnam vets like Ken Gaudet, Hugh John McCall, and Frank P. Battaglia (all veterans of the famous 173rd Airborne Division). The group's great chronicler, Robin Moore, saw in the "Crippled Eagles" an extension of the original band of Green Beret soldiers who first went out to Vietnam in order stem the tide of Asian Communism.

While not all the American volunteers in Rhodesia fought for any lofty goals other than a healthy paycheck, one certainly did. His name was John Alan Coey. Later dubbed a "martyr," Coey's reasons for fighting in Rhodesia were racial, religious, and political. In short, Coey believed that preserving White Africa in the face of Afro-Marxism and international capitalism was righteous because Rhodesia stood for Western Christendom. These views earned Coey few friends in America or even in Rhodesia, but his selfless acts of bravery helped to inspire his comrades to continue the good fight against unbelievable odds.

Born in Columbus, Ohio in 1950, Coey had all the trappings of the type of all-American life that is all but impossible to enjoy now. The Coey family wore their Lutheran faith on their sleeves and believed in one hundred percent Americanism. Coey excelled in the Boy Scouts, and when it came time to go to college, Coey decided to stay home and study forestry at The Ohio State University. So far, Coey's life contained little that was out of the ordinary.

However, one of Coey's decisions certainly marked him as unique. When he enrolled at OSU in 1968, Coey joined the officer training program for the United States Marine Corps. Coey's military aptitude earned him respect among his peers, but within the wider world of the American college campus in the late 1960s, Coey and the rest of USMC cadet-students were loathed. 1968 is the year when the Tet Offensive soured millions of Americans on the ongoing war in South Vietnam (this was due in no small part to the "fake news" of the day). Thanks to the assassinations of Bobby Kennedy and Martin Luther King, Jr., '68 has also become shorthand for political turmoil in American life. Much of this hostility came from campuses, where the New Left and the earliest stirring of popular cultural Marxism tried to convince White America that rising urban crime rates were somehow their fault for being "racist."

Coey did not buy into this programing. And yet Coey was equally distrustful of American "conservatism." For him, all of America's bluster about being the world's predominant anti-Communist power meant nothing when the country's foreign policy explicitly supported Afro-Marxist insurgents over the White-minority nations of Rhodesia, South Africa, Portuguese Angola, and Portuguese Mozambique. Coey also felt that President Richard Nixon's "Vietnamization" policy represented nothing short of cutting and running. In this way, Coey shared the same mind as Soviet dissident Aleksandr Solzhenitsyn, whose 1978 address at Harvard University denounced American politicians and anti-war students for abandoning the Vietnamese to a fate worse than death.

Coey's disenchantment with America climaxed in 1972, when, after accepting his degree, Coey dropped his Marine Corps commission and flew to Rhodesia. Here, Coey hoped to find the real fight against Communism. He would never return to the States.

Coey, who kept a diary all throughout his years in Rhodesia, let it be known that for him, the Rhodesian Bush War was all about striking against what he called the "New Order." Under the cover of free love, free choice, and multiple distractions, Coey recognized that internationalists sought to ruin everything that makes life worth living. By 1972, Coey saw that the New Left had been totally co-opted by global finance. "The left wing has recognized the dehumanizing trends of industrial society, but its activism to change society has been channeled by the real revolutionaries of Internationalism," he wrote in March 1974.[2]

Upon reading Coey's diary entries and his published articles, one gets the sense that this simple forestry student had a good working knowledge of Dissident Right authors, including maybe Oswald Spengler and Francis Parker Yockey. In other ways, Coey comes close to resembling Ernst Jünger, the former German Army officer whose experiences in World War I convinced him that a "total mobilization" of society could overcome the liberal-bourgeois cancers of capitalism and Communism. Jünger's concept of the "anarch," or the lone individual who recognizes no order but their own inner discipline, is the ultimate survivor. Like Jünger's anarch, Coey often clashed with the official line of Salisbury and had issues with the lackluster political intelligence of everyday Rhodesians. Yet, Coey's adherence to his own principles meant that he served Rhodesia with distinction, for only Rhodesia came the closest to challenging the postwar triumphalism of globalists.

Coey's independent nature would cost him a position in the legendary Rhodesian SAS. By 1973, the Rhodesian Army recognized Coey as one of their best recruits ("troopers"), and the Ohio native entered the SAS's officer selection course. Unbeknownst to the brass, Coey penned articles for Rhodesian and South African magazines under the name "Johann Coetzee." The article that really got Coey into trouble was published in October 1973 in *Assegai*, a Rhodesian Army magazine. The article expanded upon Coey's belief that the United States was a deeply anti-Western nation whose anti-Communism masked its much stronger hatred for European colonialism. The army did not take kindly to these words, and Coey lost his position in the SAS as a result.

Rather than rest or grow bitter, Coey decided to transfer to the Rhodesian Light Infantry, a commando unit that used helicopters to practice long-rang reconnaissance patrols and "fireforce" missions. Thanks to Coey and others, the position of combat medic was developed for the first time in the RLI. As the "Fighting Doc," Coey saw action all over Rhodesia's restive border with

Mozambique, the Afro-Marxist state which expelled or imprisoned all Portuguese Whites not long after achieving independence in 1975. That year would prove to be Coey's last on earth, for on July 19th, 1975, Coey was shot and killed near Mount Darwin while trying to pull another trooper to safety. His death represented the first American KIA of the Rhodesian Bush War.

It would take years for Coey's legacy to have any sort of currency beyond the confines of the Rhodesian Army. His mother tried for decades to get her son's diary published, only to receive rejection after rejection. When the diary was finally published under the title *A Martyr Speaks*, the usual lot of academics and professional book reviewers panned it as "extremist" propaganda. Black historian Gerald Horne, an avowed Marxist, labeled Coey a "white supremacist" in his book about America's involvement in the Rhodesian Bush War. Funny enough, Horne also characterized Coey as being overly paranoid about Chinese involvement in Africa, but current events have proven Coey far more in-tune with geopolitical realities than the academic Horne.

In other ways, this Christian soldier, who died at the young age of twenty-four, showed himself to be far more astute about reality than either his contemporaries or his successors. In one journal entry, Coey lambasted the American media for their foolish belief that Black rule in Rhodesia would be anything other than a total disaster. "In the eyes of the mass media the black man can do nothing wrong and white man can do nothing right, for even his sacrifices and help are discredited," Coey wrote. These words have only become truer as our civilization has devolved further.

Coey also had no time for liberal Christians who refused to see that only White Christians cared anything about preserving Christendom. One intriguing episode from Coey's diary shows his utter disdain for Evangelical and Protestant churches that worship the state of Israel more than the Gospels.

I've been going to Baptist church services. The Gospel is preached there, but I have decided to go elsewhere because these Baptists are convinced that the Zionist takeover of Palestine is the fulfillment of Biblical prophecy. They believe that the Second Coming of Christ is near, and think that they have the Revelation figured out completely. They expect to be 'raptured' away from the coming terror to help Christ rule in the Millennium. I remind them of Christ's words, "My kingdom is not of this word" and "No man knoweth the court when the Son of God shall come again."[3]

Overall, John Alan Coey can be described as a true Christian warrior of the twentieth century. More importantly, Coey's view of the world should be examined by serious students of our dissent, for Coey understood that achieving a mere "white ethnostate" is not enough. The cultural rot of liberalism can destroy even the healthiest societies. That means that breaking the grip of the New Order means creating a counter-revolution that is both about preserving the past and creating a better vision of progress. Coey did not quite hit upon Guillaume Faye's concept of "archaeofuturism," but he realized the fundamental truth that race realism without a social conservative's hatred for "free love" and secular values is doomed to recreate the same fallen society that it professes to hate.

Coey was a warrior-scholar—a representative of Jonathan Bowden's "cultured thug" class or Julius Evola's modern kshatriya. Coey was first a man of action, but he was also a man of letters who recorded fundamental truths. Most people today in the West refuse to learn these truths and will pay for such ignorance later. Let us always remember John Alan Coey, his actions, and his thoughts.

[1] Wessels, Hannes, *A Handful of Hard Men: The SAS and the Battle for Rhodesia* (Philadelphia and Oxford: Casemate, 2017), p. 123.
[2] Coey, John, *The Fighting Doc: The Rhodesian Bush War Diary of John Coey, KIA 19 July 1975* (Solihull, England: Helion & Company, 2015): 134.
[3] Ibid, 58.

Whenever there is an Islamic terror attack in the West, many citizens (usually those with a leftist bent), take to their podiums and pontificate about why the attack happened in the first place. Because they have been inundated with neo-Marxist materialism throughout their entire lives, they refuse to name the obvious, indeed the right culprit: Islam.

No, these sages, including bubblegum pop star Katy Perry, resort to empty caveats. Mental illness and racism, two conclusions that require next to no proof, tend to be favored. Other unhinged theories remove Islamist supremacism and replace it with bigger bogeymen like homophobia and misogyny. Following Omar Mateen's killing of forty-nine club goers in Orlando, journalists tripped over themselves in their race to blame Mateen's actions on his innate hatred of homosexuals. However, rather than explore Islam's official condemnation of homosexuality, reporters and talking heads latched onto highly questionable theories regarding Mateen's closeted sexuality. So far, no investigators have found any evidence that Mateen either had gay lovers or frequently visited the Pulse nightclub.

In the wake of the recent bombing in Manchester, dhimmis in the media proffered an even more ludicrous idea: the terrorist attack was carried out by a vicious woman-hater. You see, Salman Abedi, a known ISIS sympathizer who had received training in Libya and Syria, just hated little girls who had gone to the Manchester Arena in order to celebrate their burgeoning sexuality. Never mind the fact that Islam's track record with women puts Al Bundy and all other fictional misogynists to shame.

While these assertions are mostly laughable, especially given the fact that both terrorists were so clearly inspired by Islamic fundamentalism, they point to a general unwillingness in the West to take Islamic terrorism seriously. This is further compounded by public grief festivals composed of mewling, yet thoroughly un-angry crowds, and governments who spend more time cracking down on fake "hate crimes" rather than preparing deportation dockets.

However, there is one terrorism myth that is the most dangerous of all. This is the "blowback" myth, also known as "chickens coming home to roost." This theory, which is often voiced by people who should know better, sees the US and other Western nations as ultimately responsible for their own destruction. For the Europeans, the history of imperialism serves as a convenient excuse for the actions of North African and Middle Eastern terrorists, even if said terrorists have no clue about the history of British Palestine, French Algeria, or the brutal war in Indonesia after World War II.

For more US-centric voices, America's various wars in the Middle East are seen as the ultimate catalysts for terrorism across the world. The theory goes like this: if the US minded its own business, then Muslims in Iraq, Syria, and elsewhere would leave us alone. While poorly planned and executed wars in Iraq and Afghanistan have done nothing positive for the United States, they are not the reason why Muslim immigrants and their offspring keep blowing themselves up or shooting us.

Rather than listen to celebrities who cannot speak Arabic or US officials who seem to see every problem as an economic issue, we really should be listening to the terrorists themselves. As brilliantly outlined in the new book *A Paradoxical Alliance: An Anglo-American Analysis of the Left's Love Affair with Islam*, co-author Matt Palumbo quotes *Dabiq*, ISIS's magazine. According to the very men and women who seek to kill us, they hate us not because we supposedly bomb innocent Muslims throughout the world, but because we are "unbelievers."

It is really that simple: ISIS and Al-Qaeda hate the West because we have not yet submitted to Islam. Whether Christians or secularists, our refusal to follow Muhammad has sentenced us all to death. In an issue dedicated to the topic of Islamist hatred for the West, *Dabiq* writers called the American wars in the Middle East "secondary" concerns. They further added that if we pulled out of the Middle East completely, we would only earn a temporary reprieve from Islamic terrorism. No "blowback" need apply.

The myth of "blowback" is further undermined by solid data. The *International Journal of Conflict Management* found that the US's drone campaign in Pakistan, which is often characterized by liberals as the apex of US villainy abroad, actually reduces terrorism without causing any discernible "negative spillover" among the civilian population. [1] Another study by Patrick B. Johnston of the RAND Corporation and Anoop K. Sarbahi of the University of Minnesota also found that while the drone strikes are generally unpopular among civilians, they "have bolstered counter-terrorism efforts" in Pakistan. [2] Finally, Seung-Whan Choi's results in "Does U.S. Military Intervention Reduce or Increase Terrorism?" conclude that US military interventions designed to reduce terrorism (rather than produce democracy or new governments) have been predominately successful.[3]

Even without such findings, the "blowback" myth falls apart upon closer inspection. After all, Bosnia, which is a growing hotbed of jihadism, received nothing but US support during its fight against Bosnian Serbs and Croats during the 1990s. Fifty-two percent of Bosnian Muslims support the idea of Sharia law as the "revealed word of God." Strong support for Sharia law, anti-gay legislation, and honor killings can be found in countries like Malaysia, Indonesia, Bangladesh, and Niger. None of these countries have been invaded by or bombed by the US, and yet they generally support the stated aims of ISIS and Al-Qaeda.

The persistence of the "blowback" myth is the result of continued Western guilt. It allows media pundits and our elite class to continue flogging us for false sins to keep the globalist project going. If we are serious about defeating Islamic violence, then we need to get rid of this self-doubt and self-inflicted immolation. It is not working.

---

[1] Mazhar, Ummad, "Do remotely piloted aerial vehicles make terrorism more costly for terrorists?" *International Journal of Conflict Management*, Vol. 27 No. 4, 470–486.

2 Johnston, Patrick B. and Anoop K. Sarbahi, "The Impact of U.S. Drone Strikes on Terrorism in Pakistan," 21 Apr. 2015, http://patrickjohnston.info/materials/drones.pdf.
3 Choi, Seung-Wan, "Does U.S. Military Intervention Reduce or Increase Terrorism," APSA 2011 Annual Meeting Paper, 1 Aug. 2011.

Bring Back the White Man!

American Renaissance, September 30th, 2017.

The modern American college campus has so degraded words as to make them all but meaningless. The overuse and abuse of "racism" is well-documented. "Sexist" is making a hell of a run for second place these days thanks to the blue-haired harridans who teach such important topics as seventeenth-century lesbian poetry and inclusionary hip-hop.

However, one of the words that still holds real power in the world is "colonialism." In the classroom, colonialism is said with a sneer, for the word is synonymous with blue-eyed devils raping and pillaging their way towards financial gain. Outside of the walls of academe, colonialism still has negative connotations. After all, many patriotic Americans take pride in the fact that the Revolutionary War generation took up arms against a colonial power, while many lefties continue to rant against the US for its "neo-colonial" wars in the Middle East.

The anti-colonialism of academia explains why an article by Portland State professor Bruce Gilley caused such a furor. You see, Dr. Gilley, who teaches political science (which is not a science, mind you), decided to write an article entitled "The Case for Colonialism." As if that were not bad enough, the paper appeared in the *Third World Quarterly*, a scholarly journal that doles out yearly the Edward Said Award to the best apparatchiks in the field of post-colonial studies.

In case you forgot or never knew, Edward Said was a Palestinian activist who posed as a professor. His most famous work, *Orientalism*, essentially blames the West for every bad thing that ever happened. Said's main point is that the Christian West both demonizes Islam and fetishizes it.

Well, for some reason or another, the Third World Quarterly decided to publish "The Case for Colonialism," an academic treatise that lays out why colonialism has been a net good for the world, especially Africa.

The response to Gilley's article was swift and vicious.

One South African law professor characterized Gilley's piece as offensive and a form of celebration for the "Euro-American Cathedral." Several committee members of the journal not only pushed for the removal of Gilley's piece (a move that, strangely, Gilley supports), but some even requested that Gilley be stripped of his doctorate. The word "blacklist" was used once or twice.

Such reactions must be grounded in logic, right? After all, staid college professors would not tear their hair out unless the article in question was truly, undeniably inflammatory, right?

Get real!

"The Case for Colonialism" is a dangerous piece only if you have completely swallowed post-colonial dogma. Overall, Gilley's article is a nuanced, fact-filled piece that correlates nicely with common sense. The same cannot be said for the pabulum that the *Third World Quarterly* usually publishes.

"For the last 100 years, Western colonialism has had a bad name." This is how Gilley starts his argument. From here, the author points out that colonialism and the Euro-American concept of "good governance" has helped millions of people who would otherwise be living in wretched poverty. "The case for Western colonialism is about rethinking the past as well as improving the future," Gilley writes, "It involves reaffirming the primacy of human lives, universal values, and shared responsibilities."

Gilley's paper argues for more than just historical reevaluation, however. Indeed, Gilley directly argues in favor of Western nations reestablishing colonies in Africa and Asia.

Suppose that the government of Guinea-Bissau were to lease back to Portugal the small uninhabited island of Galinhas that lies 10 miles off the mainland and where the former colonial governor's mansion lies in ruins. The annual lease would be US$1 so that the Portuguese spend *their money on the island and the Guinea-Bissau government is not dependent on a lease fee. Suppose, then, that the US$10 million to US$20 million in foreign aid wasted annually on the country were redirected to this new offshore colony to create basic infrastructure.*[1]

I think that we all know what would happen—Galinhas would become not only more livable than the rest of Guinea-Bissau, but it would also be an economic hub, maybe even the most buzzing hub in all of Africa.

Such proposals, along with Gilley's call for sub-Saharan African governments to embrace colonial-style governments, is a wooden stake aimed directly at the heart of the vampire known as post-colonial theory. Direct recolonization would end the foreign aid racket that is so key to lining the pockets of Africa's many kleptocracies. Recolonization would also cause many African governments to admit that their experiments with freedom have failed and failed spectacularly.

Take for instance the aforementioned state of Guinea-Bissau. Beginning in 1963, Amilcar Cabral, a hero of the "decolonization" era, began his guerrilla campaign against the Portuguese. Gilley quotes Cabral as saying that it was "necessary to totally destroy, to break, to reduce to ash all aspects of the colonial state."[2] Cabral's long campaign, which some have called "Portugal's Vietnam," did indeed reduce the Portuguese colonial state and its institutions to ashes. In its stead, Cabral, with armament and economic support from the Soviet Union, Czechoslovakia, Cuba, and Sweden, oversaw a murderous regime that killed as many as 25,000 people and displaced 150,000. Furthermore, in 1980, Guinea-Bissau's rice production stood at 80,000 tons, a full 50 percent drop from the highpoint achieved under Portuguese rule. These days, the average resident of Guinea-Bissau is expected to live only to be fifty-five years old. Western aid and the permanent presence of UN peacekeeping troops has done very little to help.

There are of course other horror stories. Zimbabwe under Robert Mugabe became an almost laughably corrupt state where an average of $1 billion was lost every year thanks to the dictator's slimy Black supremacist politics. Watching old videos of what

Zimbabwe was like when it was called Rhodesia and was run by the White minority is akin to watching a fantasy film—one cannot believe that such a prosperous country could become such a hellhole.

South Africa is a well-known case, but it bears repeating that more Black South Africans are now killed yearly than died at the hands of the Apartheid state. There is also the case of Equatorial Guinea, which was a Spanish colony up until 1968. The first leader of an independent Equatorial Guinea was Macias Nguema, a deranged and illiterate mass murderer who killed as many as 80,000 people out of an entire population of just 300,000.[3]

Not to be outdone, The Democratic Republic of the Congo has been at war with itself since Brussels abandoned the colony in the 1960s. The Second Congo War alone killed 5.4 million people, with 45,000 dying each month in 2007.[4] Even anti-colonial hero Patrice Lumumba admitted in his autobiography that the Belgian imperialists had given the Congolese "human dignity" and helped to turn that nation "into free, happy, vigorous, and civilized men."

Such African praises for European colonialism confirm Gilley's work, from Nigerian novelist Chinua Achebe offering thanks to the British imperialists for leaving behind a prosperous and unified Nigeria, to one resident of Kinshasa who asked a foreign journalist: "How long is this independence of ours going to last anyway? When are the Belgians coming back?" It is not hard to imagine why such sentiments might be common in Africa.

Overall, Gilley's article is a clear indictment of the post-colonial racket and those gullible Western nations that continue to fall victim to the blood libel about White responsibility for Africa's plight. Such guilt helps to keep employed racist professors who specialize in useless majors. Furthermore, sub-Saharan Africans routinely invoke the sins of colonialism to squeeze money out of the West and scrounge up support among their own voters. It is better than admitting publicly that life was better under European rule. Gilley should be commended for having the decency to tell the truth in an age so thoroughly corrupted by dogma and unreason.

As Gilley notes at the end of his article, while many today may find the idea of resurrecting colonialism to be evil or "preposterous," it is not as "preposterous as the anti-colonial ideology that for the past 100 years has been haunting the lives of hundreds of millions of people."

[1] Gilley, Bruce, "The Case for Colonialism," *National Association of Scholars*, Summer 2018. https://www.nas.org/academic-questions/31/2/the_case_for_colonialism.

[2] Ibid.

[3] Wansell, Geoffrey, "True hell on earth: Simon Mann faces imprisonment in the cruelest jail on the planet," *Daily Mail*, 18 May 2007.

[4] McGreal, Chris, "War in Congo kills 45,000 people each month," *The Guardian*, 23 Jan. 2008.

One of the most pernicious lies of modern history is that the Italian soldier cannot fight. There is even a joke about it: when it comes to Jews and Italians, one wants to fight Italians in a group, but never alone. (The opposite, the joke claims, is true about Jews.) Much of this mockery comes for the objectively poor performance of the Royal Italian Army during World War II.

Compared to both the German *Wehrmacht* and the Imperial Japanese Army, the Italians were very much a junior player in the Axis. However, the bravery and stamina of the ordinary Italian soldier has been unfairly maligned by military historians who should know better. The German Field Marshal Erwin Rommel praised the Italian light infantry (known as the *Bersaglieri*) by saying: "The German soldier has impressed the world, however, the Italian Bersagliere soldier has impressed the German soldier."

Throughout World War II, Italian troops proved their mettle at the Battle of Kasserine Pass, the battles in East Africa, and their defense of their homeland in 1943. While the Fascist regime of Mussolini eventually fell, which helped to lead to the ultimate dissolution of the Italian monarchy, one cannot suspect the skill of the Italian man-at-arms.

It also bears noting that Italy's generals and its king never wanted to fight. On a practical level, the general corps knew that Italy was unprepared for a modern war—its men were exhausted and ill-trained, its factories could not compete with Britain, France, or the Soviet Union, and its economy had yet to be fully modernized. For King Victor Emmanuel III and some dedicated Fascists (most notably Marshal Italo Balbo), Italy's alliance with Nazi Germany and its implication of Nazi-style eugenic laws were anathema to Italy's mission of recreating a new Roman Empire based on the principles of Fascism.

This is not to say that Italy, whether royalist purple or Fascist black, was pacifistic. Indeed, in "The Doctrine of Fascism," Mussolini (or rather philosopher Giovanni Gentile) argued that perennial warfare was the lifeblood of the new state. King Victor Emmanuel III and the House of Savoy also gave their blessing to Italy's imperial ambitions in Africa and southeastern Europe. For European leaders in the early twentieth century, imperial conquest meant progress, both financial and cultural. Italy, like France and Great Britain, believed it had a "civilizing mission," while like the United States under President William McKinley and Theodore Roosevelt, worried that if it failed to acquire colonies, it would fall behind in the great race of geopolitics. As a result, Italian national pride meant that Italy needed a new, more professional army. This army saw action in Libya, Somalia, Eritrea, Ethiopia, Spain, and Albania, all of which occurred before the Germans crossed the border into Poland in September 1939.

Twenty-first century viewers may get a brand-new chance to watch the Italian soldier and administrator at work. Several days ago, it was reported that up to 470 Italian soldiers would be deployed to Niger. Most of these soldiers are veterans from the Iraq and Afghanistan conflicts, two battle zones that have seen Italian bullets fly and Italian bombs explode.

The Niger deployment is multi-faceted. Prime Minister Paolo Gentiloni said on December 24th that the Italian military is currently scouting out Niger to see to what degree Islamist terrorism could pose a problem. In case you forgot, several Black politicians accused President Donald Trump of explicit racism for supposedly being cold to the widow of a Black Special Forces soldier who was killed by Islamist rebels in Niger. As with most of the Sahel, Niger is home to a sizable population of Muslim bandits who owe their allegiance to Al-Qaeda and other trans-national insurgencies.

Besides combating terrorism, the deployment is also part of a plan to stop the flow of migrants to Italy. Without question, this objective is the more important one. Rome has decided that Niger is one of the major hubs of the cross-Sahara migrant route, which usually ends up in the slave markets of Libya. Although landlocked, Niger has proven to be an important port of call for the 600,000

Africans (most of them Nigerians) who have been enticed to Europe with promises of economic advancement. A large portion of these misled Nigerians wind up working as pimps and prostitutes in Italy's less developed south.

Destroying people smugglers is the explicit purpose of the Italian military mission. However, as the book *Roadmap to Hell* by Barbie Latza Nadeau makes clear, southern Italian society is being changed for the worse by Nigerian gangs and the prostitutes that they bring over. As part of this skin trade, Italian criminal organizations have made partnerships not only with West African drug lords, but also with Islamist gangs. The guns used at the Bataclan in Paris were purchased in Italy from Camorra gangsters, and the Camorra is just one of the organized crime groups in southern Italy and Sicily that is making a killing by bringing Nigerian and other African men and women to Italy. Thus, organized crime, terrorism, and globalist "humanitarianism" is linked.

However, despite the sensibility of using soldiers to enforce a nation's immigration laws, many neoliberal bleeding hearts have already described the deployment of Italian troops to West Africa as an act of colonialism. Similar calls have been raised over Italy's similar commitments to send troops to Libya and Tunisia—two former Italian colonies that are experiencing civil war and civil unrest involving Muslim terrorist gangs. In the eyes of the post-colonial (see: anti-White) left, Italian troops on African soil will produce nothing but a repeat of past injustices.

The first Italian mission to Africa was a historical failure. Only recently unified by a liberal republican army, the Kingdom of Italy sought to acquire a major colony in Africa. By the 1890s, Italy set its sight on the Christian Empire of Ethiopia—a medieval-style state ruled by an Orthodox monarchy and consisting of a mixed Christian and Muslim population. However, despite its claims of ancient ancestry, the empire was a relatively new creation. In 1889, Menelik II declared Abyssinia into being after defeating the provinces of Tigray and Amhara. At the time, the major players in East Africa were France, Britain, and the British-controlled Khedive of Egypt. However, by 1885, the Italians were vying for control of ports in East Africa that had recently been abandoned by the Egyptians. Eager to be a great power, Italy and Abyssinia signed the Treaty of Wuchale in 1889, which gave Rome control over Eritrea and certain Red Sea ports.

Because of translation issues, the Treaty of Wuchale helped to lead both countries towards war. In the Amharic edition of the treaty, the Abyssinian rulers acknowledged Italy's primacy in Eritrea. In the Italian language version, the Treaty of Wuchale agreed to turn Abyssinia into a "protectorate" of the Italian Kingdom. The Italians took this news to the great powers of Europe (Britain, France, Germany, Russia, and Austria-Hungary), and told all of them that Abyssinia was now their territory.

When Abyssinia criticized these declarations, Italian nationalists rushed to print jingoistic demands to defend Italian pride. Some Italian officials also appealed to White European unity, saying that the word of a Black kingdom means less than the word of a European state. One ardent nationalist, Prime Minister Francesco Crispi, a political left-winger who took part in the *Risorgimento*, or unification of Italy, claimed that the Horn of Africa was the best place to build a "Second Roman Empire."

Riding this wave of nationalist sentiment, the Royal Italian Army invaded Abyssinia in late 1894. The war went terribly for the Italians almost from the beginning. Thanks to a general mobilization and financial and military support from fellow Orthodox power Russia, the Abyssinian army proved numerically and tactically superior to its Italian foe. The most famous confrontation between the two forces occurred during the Battle of Adowa, which took place on March 1st, 1896.

During that battle, an Italian army led by General Oreste Baratieri decided to pursue Menelik's larger army even though they were undersupplied, lacked adequate maps, and carried defective or otherwise ill-kept rifles. At Adowa, 14,500 Italian and Eritrean soldiers squared off against 100,000 Abyssinians. Seventy percent of Baratieri's force was either killed or captured at the battle. Emperor Menelik was triumphant, and the Italians retreated to Eritrea. Eritrean soldiers loyal to Italy had their limbs hacked off by the Ethiopians. Some newspapers reported that the corpses of Italian troops were similarly mutilated. Back home, angry Italians demonstrated in the cities, and these riots had to be put down by the Italian state.

Despite this turn of events, Rome did not abandon its imperial ambitions. In 1911, Italian nationalists pressed for and got a war with the decaying Ottoman Empire. The Turks put up a whole lot of resistance (thanks in no small part to a guerrilla campaign orchestrated by Ottoman officer and future Turkish leader Mustafa Kemal), but in the end, Italy became the new ruler of most of what is today Libya. The war not only announced Italy's arrival as a major player in Europe, but it was also the first time that airpower had been used in combat.

Italy's victory in Libya would be short-lived. Thanks to World War I and the fierce fighting against the smaller, but courageous Austro-Hungarian forces that almost broke the will of the Royal Italian Army, Italian control over Libya slipped to the point where Italian forces were only in control of a thin strip of coastal land in the north.

After Benito Mussolini, a former socialist who became a patriot after serving in the Italian Army, came to power in 1922, his jingoistic foreign policy demanded that Italy reconquer the intransigent tribes of Libya. "The Pacification of Libya" was a bloody campaign that saw the use of Italian concentration camps. An ethnic cleansing of the Cyrenaican tribes only ended in 1932, when approximately 80,000 of them had perished. Muammar Gaddafi would later remind Italian Prime Minister Silvio Berlusconi of this ugly history in 2009. The Libyan leader greeted the Italian PM by wearing a picture of a captured Berber leader pinned to his uniform.

Elsewhere in Africa, Italian colonial forces got their revenge by conquering Abyssinia in 1936. Italy's first offensives went side-ways, but the Fascist government decided to use poison gas and aerial bombardments to weaken the resolve of the Abyssinians. This is often cited as the moment when the war in Europe became inevitable. After Nazi Germany left the League of Nations in unity with Italy, the ill-will between Mussolini and Hitler (an ill-will based on the Nazi-orchestrated murder of pro-Italian leader Engelbert Dollfuss in Austria) began to diminish.

As the masters of Italian East Africa, Italy built gorgeous Catholic churches, constructed highways, and improved education in the impoverished nations of Eritrea, Abyssinia, and Somalia. While laws were passed against race mixing, Italian settlers (who moved to East Africa in large numbers owing to generational poverty in rural Italy) rarely followed them. Eritreans enjoyed high standing in the colonial army, with Marshal Rudolfo Graziani, a dedicated Fascist, calling them the "Prussians of Africa." As is the case with other post-colonial societies, none of the former Italian colonies in North or East Africa have done better or been more stable since the Italians pulled out and left.

All one must do is look at Somalia and see that Italian colonization was beneficial.

While left-wing critics are correct in stating that Italian imperialists were responsible for human rights violations in North and East Africa, the history of Italy's occupation of Africa is not as villainous as it is usually depicted. The lives of Italy's African citizens improved under Rome's direction. The Royal Italian Army proved to be beneficial for Abyssinians (especially the people of Tigray) and Eritreans, many of whom learned how to read and write while in uniform. Despite what anti-colonial theorists say, Italy lost money while running its African empire, thus showing the lie behind the oft-repeated shibboleth that imperialism was all about economic exploitation. For a time, Mogadishu was a first-class city. Italians built farms, schools, and the region's first airport. The *Banca d'Italia* gave its blessing to Mogadishu by opening a branch in the city.

In Abyssinia, the Italian Duke of Aosta abolished slavery. Similar anti-slavery laws were passed in other parts of Italian East Africa.

While recent military engagements in the Third World have proved disastrous, one hopes that Italy's more limited role in Niger may help to stem the rising tide of color pouring into Europe. While American liberals may scoff at such "antiquated" fears, they have never been to Castel Volturno. Here, most of the population is Black (the largest percent from crime-ridden Nigeria) and hookers line the streets. Municipal control is non-existent, and an alliance between the Camorra and Nigerian street gangs keep the police out. As more and more migrants pour into southern Italy and Sicily, more and more small towns and cities are becoming Third World colonies.

For your usual bourgeoisie, this will only become a problem when the Amalfi Coast becomes an irredeemable pigsty. It is getting that way, and that is one reason why Italian troops are being sent into Africa. May they repeat the glories of their great-grandfathers.

Hopefully, Britain, France, Germany, and Spain follow suit. No regime change needed; just keep the migrants there.

Mexico is a failed state. Our pundits and political class will never say it out loud, but everyone this side of the Rio Grande knows it to be true. All it takes is a quick perusal of recent news headlines to support such an obvious conclusion.

In October 2019, the Mexican Army and Federal police entered the Sinaloan city of Culiacan with orders to arrest twenty-eight-year-old Ovidio Guzman, the son of the infamous Joaquin "El Chapo" Guzman. The warrants came from the US Justice Department, which wanted "El Raton" on charges of cocaine, marijuana, and meth trafficking.[1] The American and Mexican authorities also wished against all evidence to the contrary that the arrest of El Raton would somehow damage the hierarchy of the Sinaloa Cartel, which is based in Culiacan. This policy of targeted takedowns has yet to work against ISIS or Al-Qaeda, but Washington is if nothing not averse to multiplying bad decisions repeatedly.

Although the cops and soldiers got their hands on Guzman, they had to let the bad guy go because thousands of well-armed cartel militiamen flooded the city and captured strategic checkpoints. Some came in "technicals" with .50-caliber machine gun mounts, while others showed up in dirty Cadillacs armed with semi-automatic rifles and pistols. It was this rag-tag army that won the day and forced the Mexican Army to retreat *from a Mexican city!* As British journalist Ioan Grillo wrote in *Time* magazine, this was nothing less than "a mass insurrection."[2]

Less than a month later, Mexico's cartel gunmen claimed nine scalps, this time American ones. On Monday, November 4th, 2019, nine US citizens, including six children, were murdered by cartel *sicarios*, or assassins. The dead included a pair of eight-month-old twins. Even worse, some of the victims were burned alive when their vehicle was set ablaze.[3] Mexican and American authorities were quick to excuse the violence as a terrible case of mistaken identity.

Some in the American media went out of their way to blame the Langford family for the tragedy. *The New York Times* led the charge by asking why Mormons are in Mexico in the first place. Other publications followed suit. NBC writer Elizabeth Chuck thought it important to paint the Langford dead as extremists given that they belonged to a sect of Mormon fundamentalists headed by the LeBaron family.[4] Yes, one could argue that your average American reader would be titillated by stories of Mormons killing other Mormons down in Mexico, but to publish such an article two days after the murders seems questionable. More to the point, evidence indicates that the American mainstream media wants the public to focus more on the "crazy Mormon" angle than on the murders themselves.

In the meantime, Mormons are leaving Mexico in droves.[5] The cartels could not have hoped for a better outcome. The LeBarons, despite all their craziness and blood feuding, were doing a better job than the Mexican government when it came to protecting their communities. Mormons in Mexico had formed armed groups and had turned their villages into armed camps. This kept the cartels out. How did the Mexican government respond? They went after the Mormons and tried to take away their guns.

In Mexico corruption is endemic. It has been this way for ages. However, years ago, Mexico's corruption was confined to Mexico and was to be suffered only by Mexicans. Now, thanks to our lawless southern border, Mexico's problems, and indeed the problems of Central America and Africa, are increasingly our problems.

The solution is simple: close off the border with US troops (active duty and National Guard). Stricter enforcement, along with the arrest and deportation of all illegal immigrants, are the only things left that can save Anglo-America from becoming a colonized people in their own lands. With each passing year the likelihood of this coming to fruition moves further and further away. Even though most Republicans want tougher border enforcement, Leviathan in Washington is far too beholden to cheap labor and the noisy cadre of well-paid racial hucksters to let a commonsense, America First immigration policy gain anything close to steam.

Given this reality, I would like to offer another solution: the US military invasion of Mexico. Surely American troops would better serve our nation down there than in Syria, Iraq, or Afghanistan. And it is not like we do not have legitimate grievances against Mexico. According to the Drug Enforcement Agency (DEA), Mexico's cartels are flooding our country with counterfeit pills, many of which contain the toxic opioid fentanyl.[6] Fentanyl is one of the drugs responsible for the upsurge in overdose deaths that have primarily impacted the majority White states of Ohio, New Hampshire, and West Virginia. Mexican and Latino gangs are also some of the deadliest players in urban America's decades-long guerrilla campaign against law and order. MS-13, which began in Los Angeles among Salvadoran immigrants, may get most of the headlines, but groups like the Mexican Mafia, the Surenos, and Nortenos commit a high percentage of violent crime in San Francisco, Chicago, and Washington, D.C.

The Mexican government is guilty as well. Although he was excoriated by the American media for saying it, Tucker Carlson is right that Mexico has done more to interfere in US elections than any other foreign power. It is the Mexican government which encourages its people to move here, and once here, those same people shift our country leftward in terms of culture and economics.[7] It is the Mexican government that is failing to curb the narco insurgency within its own borders, and the very fact that such instability has lasted for over a decade now is, I believe, reason enough for the US to invade and clean house.

Given that our "deep state" is married to warfare and the profits that come from deploying our men and women all over the globe, an invasion and occupation of Mexico would, theoretically, satisfy their thirst. Although the "war for oil" meme was not true in the case of Iraq, Mexico, which posted 8.483 billion barrels of crude oil in 2017,[8] is awash in black gold. You would not know it though, as the Mexican government and the state-owned PEMEX (Mexican Petroleum) have turned the country from a veritable oil empire into a client of American oil interests. It would benefit both parties if Mexico's oil became America's, with the useless PEMEX divided between private American companies.

The greatest benefit of American occupation of Mexico would lie within the realm of civil society. Back in 1914, the US military proved their worth to the average Mexican in Veracruz, when, following a brief occupation of the city, Marines and sailors left behind a working sanitation system where once had been a "polluted water supply and a lack of adequate sewage."[9] Once Americans left, Veracruz fell back on its dissolute habits, with smallpox, cholera, and other diseases making a comeback.

Sanitation at gunpoint is still better than wanton disease. The same applies to governance. An American regime would be a boon to the average Mexican citizen, even an American regime circa 2019, which is shamefully more corrupt and perverse on average than New York during the blackest days of the Tammany Hall machine. An American military government would restore order on the streets and, if given carte blanche free from the interference from bureaucrats, could win the war against the cartels. At the very least the flow of drugs would be curtailed.

Finally, if used correctly, an American-occupied Mexico could be a new Australia or a Georgia under James Oglethorpe. Namely, our prisons could be thinned, and our streets scrubbed clean by forcing criminals and illegal immigrants to relocate to Mexico. Just think about it: Mexico could be our safety valve whenever there is domestic turbulence in the United States. Rather than expand police surveillance power here, just send the recalcitrant to Mexico and force them to work on military construction projects.

At the end of the day, America has a vested interest in a safe and prosperous Mexico. The better it is there, the better it is here. If we want to stop the invasion of illegal aliens, then maybe it is time that we as a country and a civilization seriously consider invading and occupying Mexico for the foreseeable future.

---

[1] Grillo, Ioan, "How the Sinaloa Cartel Bested the Mexican Army," *Time*, 18 Oct. 2019.
[2] Ibid.

[3] Radnofsky, Caroline, Alex Johnson, and Yuliya Talmazan, "At least nine Americans killed in Mexican highway ambush," *NBCNews.com*, 5 Nov. 2019.
[4] Chuck, Elizabeth, "Slain U.S. citizens were part of Mormon offshoot with sordid history," *NBCNews.com*, 6 Nov. 2019.
[5] Vigliotti, Jonathan, "Caravan of Mormons flees Mexico in wake of attack that killed 9," *CBSNews.com*, 10 Nov. 2019.
[6] "DEA issues warning over counterfeit prescription pills from Mexico," DEA, 4 Nov. 2019.
[7] Greenwood, Max, "Tucker Carlson: Mexico has interfered in US elections 'more successfully' than Russia," *The Hill*, 16 Jul. 2018.
[8] Garcia, David Alire, "Mexico oil reserves dip again as private firms begin to contribute," *Reuters*, 23 Mar. 2018.
[9] Boot, Max, *The Savage Wars of Peace: Small Wars and the Rise of American Power*, Revised Edition (New York: Basic Books, 2014): 154.

While much of the United States has been focused on the 2020 presidential election, new global conflicts have arisen which may impact international relations for the foreseeable future. One, the current war between Azerbaijan and Armenia over the Republic of Artsakh (an Armenian-majority enclave in Azerbaijan), involves major powers such as Russia, Israel, and Iran. So far, the United States, which has warm relations with both warring states, has voiced its support for a ceasefire amidst what is clearly a campaign of cultural genocide against Christian Armenians.

The other brewing conflict requires more from the US than mere peacemaking. This one is not a war yet but could devolve into what Samuel P. Huntington called the "Clash of Civilizations." On the one side is the French Fifth Republic, the descendant of the French Revolution and the symbol of state secularism. On the other is Turkey. I have been sounding the alarm about Turkey for some time now, but it bears repeating that under President Recep Tayyip Erdogan, Turkey has ceased being a US ally. Indeed, Erdogan's Turkey has become a vocal champion of Islamism in Europe and has sent its soldiers and associated mercenaries to the battlefields of Libya, Syria, and the Nagorno-Karabakh. Turkey is also the Muslim state most to blame for flooding Europe with supposed refugees since 2015. Turkey is also continuing its ancient rivalry with Greece via Muslim migrants, but as of now it appears the Greek authorities are holding the line, even in the face of Turkish provocation.

One of Greece's biggest champions in Europe is the government of French President Emmanuel Macron. France is also a traditional supporter of Armenia and the Armenians, and pro-Armenian sympathies are one of the few things that unite the French Left and Right. These facts alone would put France and

Turkey on a path towards conflict, and yet the true ignitor of the Franco-Turkish conflict was a hideous crime in a Parisian suburb. On October 16th, 2020, French middle school teacher Samuel Paty was decapitated by eighteen-year-old Chechen immigrant Abdoullakh Anzorov. Paty's murder came because of his showing satirical cartoons depicting the Prophet Muhammad to his class. Never mind that Paty gave permission for his Muslim students to leave the class, and never mind that Paty showed the cartoons not to offend but to inform his students about the power of free speech, Paty was murdered for insulting Muhammad just the same.

Following the gruesome murder (which was broadcast online for all to see and included several more conspirators), President Macron visited the crime scene and spoke the truth, calling it "a typical Islamist terrorist attack." French citizens mobilized to denounce the attack and the Islamization of French society. Islamic states saw things differently, with several banning French goods and products in their countries. President Erdogan went further than most, saying that Macron "needs some sort of mental treatment for his opinions on Islam." Tellingly, Erdogan invoking Enlightenment ideals to denounce the leader of the French, who more or less invented the Enlightenment while Ottoman Turkey was in terminal decline. "What else is there to say about a head of state (Macron) who doesn't believe in the freedom of religion and behaves this way against the millions of people of different faiths," Erdogan said.

While Erdogan played coy about Islamism's real definition of "freedom of religion," former Malaysian Prime Minister Mahathir Mohamad was blunter. Writing on Twitter, Mohamad said that Muslims have "a right to be angry and to kill millions of French people" because of the history of French colonialism in Muslim-majority countries. This incendiary tweet was followed up by incendiary actions—Muslims in London displayed their power by protesting in the thousands against France, Muslims attacked a guard protecting the French consulate in Saudi Arabia, and Turks and Azeris in France stormed through a mostly Armenian neighborhood in Lyon shouting "Allah Akbar." The apex of the recent violence was reached when a Tunisian immigrant named Brahim al-Aouissaoui, who had only been in Europe since

September of this year, entered the Notre Dame Basilica in Nice and murdered three worshippers. One of the dead, a sixty-year-old woman, was practically beheaded by her feral killer. The other victims were a fifty-five-year-old devout Catholic named Vincent Loques and Brazilian immigrant Simone Barreto Silva, forty-four.

So far, Macron has responded to these outrages by vowing to crackdown on Islamic extremism and support the French tradition of state secularism. The man who was elected to maintain the center-left status quo against the hard-right Marine Le Pen in 2017, and who has moved increasingly to the right in order to keep up with the French electorate, is now likely far to the left of the average French voter. Macron's relatively mild stance is not enough and will never be enough. Islamism's war against France and French culture has been extreme and extremely bloody—the murders at *Charlie Hebdo*, the Bataclan massacre, the Nice truck attack, the Christmas market attack in Strasbourg. Following the murders at the Notre Dame Basilica, French security services admitted that they foiled several planned Islamist attacks all across the country. This has gone on for too long and must end unless France desires to be in a permanent state of emergency.

Erdogan's Turkey is openly hostile to the West and its Christian heritage. Erdogan also thumbs his nose at the secularism so near and dear to the center-left in Paris. This aggression needs to be checked by a strengthened Franco-American alliance. France is America's oldest ally, and the sister republics need to do more to check Neo-Ottoman expansionism. First, Washington needs to separate entirely from Turkey. The US should instead cultivate a strong alliance with Greece and use its considerable weight to break Israel's bond with Azerbaijan, the largest vassal of Erdogan's empire. The US should encourage the French army and navy to step up operations against Turkish and Turkish-aligned forces across the Mediterranean.

Furthermore, American foreign policy should tentatively embrace Russia, which is Turkey's arch-nemesis. Backing Russian counter-offensives against Turkey would be ideal, but the current Russophobia Washington elites and the two parties that they control means that a better course of action would be to let Russia damage Turkey by itself without interference or censure. Turkey is more of a threat to the United States and our interests in the Middle East and Africa than Moscow. It is that simple.

As for France, it is long past time to realize that state secularism cannot co-exist with Islam, moderate or extreme. The *banlieues* are jihadist emirates within the Fifth Republic, and, as journalist David Thomson writes in *The Returned*, every liberal intellectual's attempt to dispute the violent heart of political Islam breeds more violent Islamists.[1] In a perfect scenario the French would return to their mother church in droves. But barring that, Paris needs to pass an immigration moratorium and consider the possibility of repatriation for all suspected extremists and/or criminals of foreign origin. If Macron's government is unwilling to do any of this, then he needs to be voted out or immediately replaced by someone with the fortitude and courage of De Gaulle or Saint Louis.

The future for the French does not look rosy, but this is the civilization that produced Charlemagne, Napoleon, and the men who withstood hell at Verdun and Fort Vaux. The US under President Donald Trump needs to remind Macron and the French government of this heroic legacy. If need be, the US should provide even more than mere words of encouragement. After all, our fight against ultra-leftist terrorism in the US is the same as France's battle against Islamism. Both forces represent the demonic and are a threat to Western civilization.

---

[1] Thomson, David, *The Returned: They Left to Wage Jihad, Now They're Back*, Trans. Gregory Flanders (Cambridge: Polity Press, 2018): 87.

THE STATE OF THINGS

If nothing else, this book is a small attempt to rekindle something that has been lost in the European soul through too much peace, too much security, and too many distractions. Our history is a glorious one, and the halcyon days of European and American imperialism were bright stars in a constellation of great luminescence. The stories told here remind us of this history—its many sacrifices, triumphs, tragedies, and ultimate victories. Let no man nor organization tell you to apologize or atone for this history. We have nothing to be ashamed of. The only shame we should have is our failure to live up to the standards set by the heroes of the Rif or the backwoods militiamen of witch-haunted New England.

Not long ago, when our grandparents were young, European men still ruled the world. The Union Jack flew high in places as disparate as Belize and Bhutan. The French tricolor hung in the casbah of Algiers. Everywhere in the world, from steaming jungles to arid deserts, the footprints of White giants could be found.

These footsteps are no more. The European empires died during the Cold War. Many were thrown away by governments eager to save money, but even more eager to conform to the new world order of 1945. After World War II, the world's two superpowers both supported anti-imperialist policies. While the Soviets denounced imperialism as bourgeois and capitalist, the United States invoked democracy and national self-determination to undermine what was left of the British, French, Dutch, and Belgian empires.

Despite all the chest thumping and saber rattling about Soviet Communism, the United States gladly gave aid to openly Marxist movements in Africa. The strongest anti-Communist states on the continent, Rhodesia and South Africa, received American opprobrium for their adherence to White-minority rule. President

Jimmy Carter, "who made the human rights agenda a particular priority for his administration," reversed the Nixon administration's support for White Africa's anti-Communist fight to achieve geopolitical balance with the Soviet Union.[1] Carter's focus on the mythical fetish of "human rights" resulted in the loss of Rhodesia, the birth of Zimbabwe, and the eventual looting and murder of White farmers. Rhodesia was once the breadbasket of Africa. Now it is a wasteland where money is of little value and human life is worth less.

The policies of the liberal Democrat Carter continued during the administration of the supposedly conservative Republican Ronald Reagan. Although President Reagan vetoed the bill, the Comprehensive Anti-Apartheid Act passed the Senate in 1986 with eighty-one Republican votes, thereby overriding the Gipper.[2] White South Africa—the true and only civilization of South Africa—limped on for a few more years before being swallowed up by the unholy alliance of Afro-Marxism and Western liberalism. These days, South Africa is synonymous with violent crime, endemic corruption, and ghastly farm murders that see innocent White families raped, hacked, slashed, stabbed, and even burnt alive by mostly Black assailants.

While European imperialism expired on the Dark Continent decades ago, imperialism is still very much with us. These days, the descendants of the hardy frontiersmen, colonial soldiers, and settlers chronicled in this book are themselves subjected to imperialist oppression. Governments across Western Europe and North America do not represent their own people. Our governments are foreign occupiers even though the leaders may have American or British passports. These governments denigrate the native White population. They flood streets built by our forebearers with foreign peoples who do not share our language, culture, religion, or race. Our imperial overlords tell us to hate ourselves. They force our soldiers, sailors, Marines, and airmen to attend anti-White indoctrination sessions. Every day they kill the innocence of our youth by poisoning their minds with vile dogma about the "evil" of "whiteness." Their goal is obvious—the destruction of White identity and European civilization by any means necessary.

We in the West find ourselves in this unenviable position, but it is not a hopeless one. Our ancestors fought like wild beasts for less noble goals, so it stands to reason that we can fight like hell for the only goal that matters—the preservation of our civilization. To do so, we must study the anti-imperialist movements of the past. We need to study how they organized as political cadres, as paramilitary units, and as radicals motivated by a single goal. The cryto-Communist journalist Robert Taber once dubbed guerrilla warfare the "war of the flea." Fleas cannot kill their host, but they can exhaust it and drain it enough that it quits the field. We, the occupied natives of North America, Europe, South Africa, Australia, and New Zealand, can fight like the fleas and deny the occupiers our blood, sweat, and money. We can fortify redoubts in the small towns and villages of the interior; we can establish what Kai Murros calls base areas in cities that will be "islands inside the deteriorating liberal-capitalist system." [3] These base areas will include well-dressed and well-armed men motivated by in-group preference and a desire to protect that inheritance. These base areas are not meant to reconquer a city or cities, but rather form sharp impediments to state or non-state abuse from our enemies. Belfast nearly exhausted the British Army during the Troubles; hundreds of Belfasts could easily drain the American juggernaut.

The coming years will be uncomfortable. Life under occupation is never comfortable. However, if we get serious about organizing and about living in ways that honor the men who came before us, then nothing can stop us. We can and will replace the venal empire of the liberal elite with a new empire of our own creation. This empire will be based on tradition, kin, and masculinity. There will be conquests. There will be gold and other treasures. But, before we can reach the next age of Occidental greatness, we must first fight and win the ultimate struggle for our survival.

The war is now.

---

[1] Michel, Edward R., "The White House and White Africa: Presidential Policy on Rhodesia, 1965–1979," Ph.D. Diss., (University of Birmingham, 2016).

[2] Redden, Jr., Thomas J., "The US Comprehensive Anti-Apartheid Act of 1986: Anti-Apartheid or Anti-African National Congress?," *African Affairs*, Vol. 87, No. 349 (Oct. 1988): 596–599.

[3] Murros, Kai, *Revolution and How to Do It in Modern Society*, 4, http://www.kolumbus.fi/aquilon/revolution.pdf.